AA Explore
SCOTLAND

Dochart Falls, Killin, near the shores of Loch Tay

AA Publishing

Text and illustrations taken from the series *Explore Britain's...*, first published by the Automobile Association and the Daily Telegraph in 1993 and 1995:

Explore Britain's Castles by Elizabeth Cruwys and Beau Riffenburg
Explore Britain's Coastline by Richard Cavendish
Explore Britain's Country Gardens by Michael Wright
Explore Britain's Historic Houses by Penny Hicks
Explore Britain's National Parks by Roland Smith
Explore Britain's Steam Railways by Anthony Lambert
Explore Britain's Villages by Susan Gordon

Published by AA Publishing, a trading name of Automobile Association Developments Limited, whose registered office is Norfolk House, Priestley Road, Basingstoke, Hampshire RG24 9NY. Registered Number 1878835.

A catalogue record for this book is available from the British Library.

ISBN 0 7495 1304 7

Colour origination by L.C. Repro & Sons Ltd, Aldermaston, England
Printed and bound in Italy by Tipolitografia G. Canale & C.S.p.A. – Turin

Acknowledgements:

AA PHOTO LIBRARY B/Cover: a K. Paterson, b J. Henderson, c D. Forss, d S. L. Day, f R. G. Elliott; 1 H. Williams, 3, 7, 8/9 S. L. Day; 8 K. Paterson; 9a, 9b S. L. Day; 10 J. Beazley; 11 M. Alexander; 12/13, 13 J. Beazley; 14 S. & O. Mathews; 15, 16 J. Beazley; 17 M. Taylor; 18, 19 J. Beazley; 20 M. Alexander; 21 J. Beazley; 22 S. & O. Mathews; 23 J. Beazley; 24/5, 25 D. Hardley; 26, 27 M. Taylor; 28, 29, 30/1; 31 K. Paterson; 32 S. Gibson Photography; 34 J. Carnie; 35 P. Sharp; 36/7, 37 J. Beazley; 38/9, 39 E. A. Bowness; 41 J. Beazley; 42 D. Hardley; 43 J. Beazley; 44 P. Sharp; 45 D. Corrance; 46 K. Paterson; 47 M. Taylor; 48/9 J. Beazley; 49, 50, 51 D. Corrance; 52 F. Raffles; 53 D. Corrance; 54, 55 R. Weir; 56/7, 57, 58, 59 K. Paterson; 60 M. Taylor; 61 S. L. Day; 62 J. Carnie; 63, 64 M. Taylor; 65 J. Carnie; 66 R. Weir; 67 J. Beazley; 68/9, 69 M. Alexander; 70, 71 M. Alexander; 72 A. Baker; 73 S. L. Day; 74 P. Sharp; 75 R. Weir; 76 J. Henderson; 77 J. Beazley; 78/9 R. Weir; 80 J. Henderson; 81 R. Weir; 82 S. L.Day; 83 K. Paterson; 84 S. L. Day; 85 P. Sharp; 86, 87 J. Henderson; 88 M. Taylor; 89 R. Weir; 90/1 J. Henderson; 92, 93 S. L. Day; 94 R. Weir; 95 E. Ellington; 96, 97, 98/9, 99 R. Weir; 100, 101 J. Beazley; 102 M. Taylor; 103 J. Beazley; 104/5, 105 J. Henderson; 106 M. Taylor; 108 J. Carnie; 109 R. Weir; 110, 111 E. Ellington; 112, 114/5 M. Taylor; 115 J. Beazley; 116, 117 M. Taylor; 118 R. G. Elliott; 120 J. Carnie; 121 J. Beazley; 122 J. Carnie; 123 K. Paterson; 124/5 R. Weir; 126, 127 A. Grierly
ANDY WILLIAMS PHOTO LIBRARY F/Cover Eilean Donan Castle

Contents

SCOTLAND

N
Holborn Head
John o' Groats
Scourie
Ardvreck Castle
Dunrobin Castle
Bonar Bridge
Duntulm Castle
Gairloch
Dunvegan Castle
Shieldaig
Isle of Skye
Plockton
Eileen Donan Castle
Urquhart Castle
Strathspey Railway
Portsoy
Cawdor Castle
Huntly Castle
Peterhead
Kildrummy Castle
Tolquhon Castle
Craigievar Castle
Castle Fraser
Braemar
Balmoral
Crathes Castle
Dunnottar Castle
Blair Castle
Edzell Castle
House of Dun
Strontian
Glamis Castle
House of Pitmuies
Castle Stalker
Mull and West Highland Railway
Torosay Castle
Killin
Scone Palace
Claypotts Castle
Huntingtower
Iona
Taynuilt
Kilchurn Castle
Castle Campbell
Falkland Palace
Hill of Tarvit
St Andrews Castle
Innis Connel Castle
Forth Rail Bridge
Loch Leven
Pittenweem
Lower Largo
Elie
Kilmartin
Crinan
Crarae Gardens
Stirling Castle
Culross
Kinghorn
Dirleton Castle
Hopetoun House
Cramond
Tantallon Castle
Bo'ness and Kinneil Railway
Lauriston Castle
Plants from the Past
Linlithgow Palace
Edinburgh Castle
St Abbs
Bothwell Castle
House of the Binns
Craigmillar House
Mellerstain
Floors Castle
New Lanark
Neidpath Castle
Abbotsford
Traquair House
Brodick Castle
Ayr
Wanlockhead
Culzean Castle
Hermitage Castle
Caerlaverock
Portpatrick
Dunskey
Orchardton Tower
0 10 20 30 40 50 miles
0 20 40 60 80 km

INTRODUCTION

Mourn, hapless Caledonia, mourn
Thy banish'd peace, thy laurels torn!

Tobias George Smollett, 'The Tears of Scotland'

Scotland consists of the finest wilderness areas in Britain. With its mountains, glens, lochs and stunning landscapes it could be thought of as one enormous national park. It is surprising, therefore, that, unlike England and Wales, Scotland has no designated National Parks. However, lack of official designations in no way detracts from the beauty and drama the region.

Think of Scotland and we imagine warrior clans, castles and whisky. But there is also a gentler side manifested in gardens such as Brodick on the isle of Arran, parts of which are medieval; or what about Crarae Gardens, a 'Himalayan ravine' created in the highland glen, with its ancient chambered tomb. Then there is the colourful contrast of 'Plants from the Past', recreating the splendour of an 18th century garden.

Few places in Scotland are very far from the sea, a feature reflected in the history, social character and economics of the country. Scots originated with 6th century seaborne Irish invaders of Argyll who eventually united with the Picts of the east. Viking raiders settled in the north and west, and Orkney and Shetland remained under Norse rule until the 15th century. Naturally the inhabitants depended on fishing for food, with smuggling rife both east and west from Ireland and northern Europe. Scotland's deeply contoured coastline, including almost 800 islands, is one of contrasts: stark cliffs, harbours offering

O Caledonia! stern and wild,
Meet nurse for a poetic child!
Land of brown heath and shaggy wood,
Land of the mountain and the flood,
Land of my sires! what mortal hand
Can e'er untie the filial band
That knits me to thy rugged strand!

From Sir Walter Scott's 'The Lay of the Last Minstrel'

Kilchurn Castle, looking towards Beinn Eunaich and, right, the Edinburgh Festival

fast routes to Ireland, north west England and north Wales; sandy beaches and some of the best and most famous links golf courses in the world; sea lochs; spectacular mountains and an eastern coast less dramatic but with former fishing ports serving as holiday resorts and retirement centres.

Each region of Britain naturally has its own distinctive community feel but, unlike in England, and, to a certain extent, in Wales, Scottish villages have not revolved around the village green. Indeed, robbed of their traditional livelihood, many communities, like the crofters of 19th century Scotland, were forced to abandon their villages. Even so, the remaining villages are rich in history and character.

For many centuries no important house was built in the borders without fortification, a feature which gives Scotland's historic houses added drama and mystique. Among them is Balmoral, one the world's most famous stately homes.

Below, on guard at Glenfinnan Station, deep in the Highlands

Left, window detail from Claypotts Castle, near Dundee

Which brings us to one of the underlying features of Scotland – its castles, proudly defending the borders from raids by both Scots and English for centuries. Over thirty of the finest are included in this compilation, leaving many more to explore. Although many now lie in ruins, many are still remarkably intact and some, like Glamis, family home of the Queen Mother and birthplace of Princess Margaret, have been occupied almost continuously. Whether ancient and ruins or relatively modern constructions, there are few more inspiring sights than one of Scotland's many castles, imposing itself on the landscape or rising majestically from the security of the lochs.

Abbotsford stands on the site of the last of the clan battles in the Borders, a fact which is wholly in keeping with Sir Walter Scott's romantic view of historical events and which may even have influenced his choice of a new home.

ABBOTSFORD

Borders

2 MILES (3.2 KM) WEST OF MELROSE

Abbotsford is fascinating on two counts – first because it was the home of Sir Walter Scott, and second because of the diverse collections with which the writer filled his house. Many of these collections were brought with him from his former home, just a few miles away at Ashiestiel, and it is said to have been a curious procession which moved up the valley to Abbotsford on 28 May 1812. By this time Sir Walter was already a published writer, with the profits from *The Lay of the Last Minstrel, Marmion* and *The Lady of the Lake* contributing to the purchase of his new home. Two years after moving in he began his *Waverley* series of novels, and as his success as a writer grew, so too did Abbotsford and its estate.

Sir Walter Scott's lovely mansion on the River Tweed is a reminder of a great man

In 1818 the former farmhouse was extended by the addition of an armoury, a dining room, a study, a conservatory and three extra bedrooms. Then in 1822 the original building was demolished to make way for what is now the main block of Abbotsford. By this time Sir Walter's holdings of land had increased to some 1,400 acres (567ha), which he liberally planted with trees. The house was further extended in the 1850s by Sir Walter's descendant, Walter Lockhart Scott, who added a west wing containing the chapel and kitchen, thus completing the attractive composition we see today.

Successive generations of Scotts have made Abbotsford their home, but it remains a splendid memorial to their famous ancestor and all around the house are reminders of him. The study is particularly evocative, with a bronze cast of his head still watching over his writing desk, and shelves and shelves of books which have spilled over from the library. Altogether there are about 9,000 volumes collected by Sir Walter. He looks out over the drawing room, too, from the famous portrait by Raeburn over the fireplace. This is a delightful room, with the Chinese hand-painted wallpaper given to Sir Walter by his cousin, and a roll-top desk and chairs given to him by George IV.

Sir Walter had a fascination for historic weaponry, and his armoury contains an interesting mixture ranging from his own blunderbuss to Rob Roy's broadsword, dirk and sporran purse. Bonnie Dundee's pistol is here, and the double-barrelled carbine of a Tyrolean patriot.

Other curiosities are dotted around the house, including various relics from the Battle of Waterloo, two cannon balls from the siege of Roxburgh Castle in 1460, a model of the skull of Robert the Bruce and a 'scold's bridle', used to silence nagging wives.

Open from late March to October daily. Tel: 01896 2043.

Above and right, the largest mansion in Scotland to be inhabited, Floors Castle is set in pleasant gardens above the River Tweed

FLOORS CASTLE

Borders

1 MILE (1.5 KM) NORTH OF KELSO

Floors Castle is enormous – indeed, it is the largest inhabited house in Scotland. It was built in the early 18th century for the 1st Duke of Roxburghe, who played a leading part in the union of Scotland with England in 1707. Doubtless the situation of his home in the Borders coloured his views, for this was a troubled frontier of cross-border skirmishes and moving boundaries for many centuries before the two countries united.

The castle's architect was William Adam, but his creation was enlarged and embellished about a century later by William Playfair, whose many other commissions included the National Gallery in Edinburgh. It was he who added the countless pepper-pot cupolas which give Floors its fairy-tale appearance today. By this time the 6th Duke was in residence, having inherited the title and the estate at the age of just seven years. He was the heir of Sir James Innes,

who had won the inheritance after a protracted and very expensive court case during which a number of distant relatives claimed the dukedom. Sir James was 76 years old and childless when he was granted the title and the estate, encouraging many of his unsuccessful rivals to wait eagerly in the wings for a second chance. However, in his 80s he fathered a son, James – the 6th Duke. James both increased the family fortunes and its importance to such an extent that he was honoured with a state visit from Queen Victoria in 1867 – a summer-house in the garden was built especially for her.

Though the exterior of the castle has changed little since the 6th Duke's day, the interior was considerably altered by the 8th Duke around the turn of the century. For the contents we must largely thank his wife, the American heiress Mary Goelet, who devoted herself to the house she had been taken to as a bride in 1903. From her Long Island home she brought the wonderful collection of 17th-century Brussels tapestries which adorn the walls of Floors Castle, and she also acquired the collections of French furniture and contemporary art which enhance the elegant rooms here. The Needle Room, reputedly identical to a room at Versailles, now acts as a gallery for paintings by Matisse, Redon, Bonnard and Augustus John.

The gardens and grounds around Floors Castle are delightful; they contain a holly tree which is said to mark the spot where James II was killed whilst besieging the castle.

Open at Easter, then from late April to October on selected days, but daily in high summer. Tel: 01573 223333.

'... altogether a kingdom for Oberon and Titania to dwell in.'
Sir Walter Scott

Floors Castle was seen world-wide when it appeared as the ancestral home of Tarzan, in the film *Greystoke*

MELLERSTAIN

Borders

3 MILES (5 KM) SOUTH OF GORDON

This grand and imposing mansion, home of the Earl and Countess of Haddington, was built in two stages – the first by William Adam in 1725 and the second by his more famous son, Robert, in the 1770s.

Although the house is 18th-century through and through, the ancestors of the current Earl and Countess, the Baillies, had owned the estate since 1642. Mixed fortunes in the early years led various members of the family into imprisonment, exile and execution. However, a young and penniless George Baillie fled to Holland to become a junior officer in the Prince of Orange's Horse Guards. When that same Prince of Orange became William III of England, the family fortunes were restored so they were in a position to create this beautiful home, which has been splendidly preserved in its original style.

The classical interiors are among the finest you will see anywhere – the library has justifiably been hailed as a masterpiece – and the intricate plaster ceilings and panels are exquisite. Elegant furniture and fine paintings more than adequately set off the design and decoration of each of the rooms, and as well as many family portraits the house contains works by Van Dyck, Gainsborough, Ramsay, Aikman and Nasmyth.

Open over Easter, then from May to September daily, except Saturday. Tel: 01573 410225.

Pleasing Adam interiors are a major feature of Mellerstain

The mellow old house of Traquair began its existence as a royal hunting lodge

TRAQUAIR HOUSE

Borders

1 MILE (1.5 KM) SOUTH OF INNERLEITHEN

Traquair is the oldest inhabited house in Scotland, and it is also among the most romantic. It was built in the 12th century and has been visited by no less than 27 monarchs over the years – William the Lion held court here, and there are particularly strong links with Mary, Queen of Scots and with the Jacobite cause. During the Civil War the then Earl could not quite decide which side to support, and so took no active part himself, but he sent his son to join his kinsman Montrose before the battle of Philiphaugh. Shortly afterwards, however, when the fleeing Montrose sought refuge at Traquair, the Earl pretended he wasn't at home.

The house reflects every moment of its 800 years of history, with ancient stone walls, a 'modern' wing, dating from 1680, and furniture and contents which span many centuries. The Museum Room is particularly absorbing, with items ranging from Mary, Queen of Scots' rosary and crucifix to a 16th-century calculator and a lengthy list (in her own hand) of the 4th Countess's children.

Traquair remains at the heart of a working estate which includes Britain's oldest surviving working brewery, revived to full working order in 1965.

Open Easter week, then from May to September daily. Tel: 01896 830785.

The large Bear Gates, once the main entrance to Traquair, were closed in 1745, not to be re-opened until there was once again a Stuart on the throne. Ever since that day a new drive to the house, running parallel to the old avenue, has been used.

The wind through the rusted iron sings,
The sun on the self-sown tangle burns,
But never a hoof on the roadway rings -
The gate is shut till the King returns.'

W H Ogilvie

The river that runs near the castle is known as Hermitage Water. Some 600 feet (183m) away from the castle, on the banks of the river, stand the remains of the medieval hermitage which gave Hermitage Castle its name.

HERMITAGE CASTLE

Borders

HERMITAGE, 15 MILES (24 KM) SOUTH OF HAWICK

Great walls of dark sandstone loom menacingly across the Borders, and Sir Walter Scott noted that even in his time the local people regarded this brooding fortress 'with peculiar aversion and terror'.

The merest glance explains why, for the walls rise sheer and imposing from among the grassy earthworks, and windows are few and far between. The only significant openings are the rows of doors on the very top part of the castle, which afforded access to the wooden fighting balcony that once protruded from the walls. The tower was developed from a simple 13th-century rectangular building to the grim fortress that can be seen today, by the Douglas family in the late 14th century. One of the two great flying arches was reconstructed in the 19th century, but, all in all, Hermitage today appears much as it would have done in the 15th century.

Several of Hermitage's owners committed foul deeds within its walls. One drowned a colleague near the castle, but was later boiled alive for his misdeeds, which included witchcraft. Another starved his enemies to death in the pit dungeons, although he too met an unpleasant end, murdered in a nearby forest. And Hermitage was also where Mary, Queen of Scots rushed to be at the bedside of her ailing lover, the Earl of Bothwell.

Open April to September, daily, and winter weekends. Tel: 0131 668 8800.

Its lonely setting and violent past give Hermitage Castle an eerie atmosphere

The massive tower and turrets of Neidpath Castle rise dramatically from the rock above the River Tweed

NEIDPATH CASTLE

Borders

JUST WEST OF PEEBLES

After Scotland had won her independence from England in the 14th century under great warriors like William Wallace and Robert the Bruce, local land-owners had the task of establishing law and order in their domains. Castles such as the one at Neidpath were built, not only to provide a form of defence, should the laird come under attack, but also so that he could maintain a tighter control over his subjects.

Neidpath's L-plan tower was built in the second half of the 14th century, and the upper two floors were re-modelled in the 17th century. The tower is unusual, because both arms of the L form parallelograms, rather than rectangles as was most common, and the corners are rounded. It is an intriguing building, its four main floors intersected with mural passages and 'entresols', or mezzanine floors, giving the impression that the castle is full of small chambers and passages, all at different heights.

The lower floor contained a pit prison and a well, while on the second floor is a room with some fine 17th-century panelling. Mary, Queen of Scots and James I and VI are both known to have stayed at Neidpath, although the castle has been too much altered since the 16th century to be able to identify which rooms they occupied.

Open Easter weekend, then from May to mid October daily. Tel: 01721 720333.

PORTPATRICK

Dumfries & Galloway

6 MILES (10 KM) SOUTH OF STRANRAER

What Gretna Green was to runaway English couples, so was Portpatrick to eloping lovers from Ireland – a place where they could be married with no inconvenient questions asked. Until 1826 the Church of Scotland ran a profitable trade in quick and easy weddings here: 'landed on Saturday, called on Sunday, married on Monday', as the saying went. The Rhinns Peninsula at Scotland's south-west corner is the closest point to Ireland, and Portpatrick was the Scottish end of the 21-mile passage to Donaghadee in Ulster. The mails to Ireland took this route, while Irish cattle in bellowing thousands came the other way. The snag was that Portpatrick's harbour lay at the mercy of the savage south-westerly gales. A pier was built in the 1770s, but it was not adequate and new harbour works on a massive scale began in 1820. The sea swept them all contemptuously away, and in 1849 the packet boats carrying mail, cargo and passengers to Ireland were transferred to nearby Stranraer. Portpatrick was left to develop as a pleasant small resort for sailing, sea-fishing, and nowadays watersports. The 17th-century church has an unusual Irish-style round tower, and the graveyard is the final resting place of many who died in shipwrecks on this harsh coast.

Portpatrick and its rocky harbour, seen from the southern cliffs

ST ABBS

Borders

12 MILES (19 KM) NORTH OF BERWICK

St Abb (Ebba or Aebbe) was the daughter of Edifred, King of Northumbria. Legend has it that she went to sea to escape the attentions of the king of Mercia, was shipwrecked and washed up hereabouts. In gratitude for her safe delivery (from the shipwreck, that is, not the king), she founded a double monastery-nunnery, and governed it as the abbess until she died in AD683. St Cuthbert visited her in 661. The abbey buildings were destroyed, probably by the Vikings, though there are some remains of a later foundation in her name a mile or so inland. The village lived by its fishing (and its smuggling) for centuries; lobster and crab boats still operate from here, but now it is also a holiday village, with one of the few sandy beaches on this spectacular stretch of cliff-bound coast. It clings to the cliffs, some houses looking down from the top, another group of old fishermen's cottages (now holiday homes) lower down, overlooking the little harbour and lifeboat station. Beside the harbour is a picturesque row of ageing wooden net-huts used for storing fishermen's gear. The whole place is brightly coloured, with the orangey-red of pantiled roofs set off by the mix-and-match colours of the painted stone walls of the terraced houses.

Looking down on to the harbour and the lifeboat station

St Abb's Head, just to the north of the village, is a National Nature Reserve, noted particularly for its nesting seabirds, including guillemots, razorbills, kittiwakes, shags, fulmars and eiders. The walk out there from the village along the cliffs, with the North Sea pounding below, is a spectacular one. Alternatively, the coxswain of the lifeboat runs trips to the point.

CAERLAVEROCK CASTLE

Dumfries & Galloway

CAERLAVEROCK, 12 MILES (19 KM) SOUTH-EAST OF DUMFRIES

The imposing gatehouse at Caerlaverock Castle is so similar to those designed by Edward I's master castle-builder, James of St George, that it is often suggested that this was an English, rather than a Scottish, fortress. The high walls, with their massive round towers, two moats and high ramparts, are very similar to the concentric castles built by Edward in Wales, such as Beaumaris and Harlech; but, unlike any other castle in Britain, Caerlaverock is triangular. It has three walls, two protected by an arm of the sea that swings out round the back of the castle, and the third by moats, earthworks, and the great gatehouse.

Caerlaverock was built in the late 13th century, and exchanged hands several times when Edward invaded Scotland. Edward laid siege to it in 1300, after which it was besieged another four times during its eventful history. Often, if the Scots took a castle but were unable to hold it, they would destroy it so that the English could not use it. This happened to Caerlaverock in 1312, and it was almost completely rebuilt in the 15th century. Rebuilding followed the previous plan, although gun ports were added, and the great gatehouse was strengthened to withstand cannonfire.

Open all year, daily except Christmas and New Year. Tel: 0131 668 8800.

The Renaissance walls and carved stone panels still remain at Caerlaverock

Dunskey, lying just south of Portpatrick, occupies a spectacular coastal location

DUNSKEY CASTLE

Dumfries and Galloway

6 MILES (10 KM) SOUTH-WEST OF STRANRAER

Little is known of this ruined tower house standing on a rocky peninsula that juts out into the sea. A castle is mentioned in records dating to 1330, but was burned down early in the 15th century. A new tower was raised by William Adair of Kinhilt, but this was deserted in the middle of the 17th century, and little more than a ruin by 1684.

Dunskey is a simple L-plan tower house, with cellars, a ground floor and a first floor. Walls were built around the small peninsula, so that the castle would have been surrounded by two lines of defence: firstly the sea and ditches hewn from the rock, and secondly, the walls. Virtually nothing remains of these walls, although there are traces of other buildings in what would have been the courtyard.

It is likely that Dunskey Castle would once have been a fine, proud house. The windows and doors were once decorated with dressed stones, but these, being expensive and much in demand for building, have been stripped away over the centuries by local looters. It is the absence of these stones that gives the roofless walls of Dunskey Castle their forlorn, rugged appearance.

Open access at any reasonable time.

ORCHARDTON TOWER

Dumfries & Galloway

PALNACKIE, 4½ MILES (7 KM) SOUTH OF DALBEATTIE

Of all the small tower houses and castles built in 15th century Scotland, Orchardton is one that gives the visitor a clear impression of what domestic life must have been like in Scottish medieval feudal society. The rooms inside the tower are small, cramped and dark, with narrow windows, which perhaps would have made for warmer living quarters – they certainly would have made the tower more secure from attack. But during winter, with the shutters firmly closed against the cold and a smoking fire in the hearth, Orchardton Castle would not have been a cheerful dwelling.

Orchardton is unusual because it is the only round tower house in Scotland. It was built in the mid 15th century by the Provost of Lincluden.

The basement had a vaulted roof, and unlike the other floors, is rectangular. The narrow spiral staircase is in the thickness of the wall, and rises to the top of the 33-foot (10m) high tower, where there is a gabled watchtower. Like Norman keeps, the entrance was on the first floor, so that the wooden steps which gave access to the tower could be drawn up inside the building during times of danger.

Open access at all reasonable times. Tel: 0131 668 8800.

Built by John Cairns, Orchardton Tower is the only circular tower house left standing in Scotland

WANLOCKHEAD

Dumfries & Galloway

6 MILES (9.5 KM) NORTH-EAST OF SANQUHAR

A Lowlands village, this, but one that has the distinction of being the highest in all of Scotland. It is 1531ft (465m) above sea level, set in the rounded green and brown Lowther Hills. In the 17th century these hills were the hiding-place of the Presbyterian Covenanters, persecuted so mercilessly in the cause of religious freedom. Now sheep graze free-range, even in the village itself. Many of the village's whitewashed stone houses are around the head of Wanlock Water. Most of the single-storey cottages were built between the mid-18th and the mid-19th centuries, the homes of miners, for between 1680 and 1934 the villagers lived by lead mining – though gold and silver too have been mined in the area since Roman times. The story of the local mines is told in the Museum of Lead Mining, where visitors can go on a tour of an 18th-century lead mine, a smelt mill and miners' cottages furnished in the styles of 1740 and 1890. Also here is the Miners' Reading Society Library, founded in 1756 and the second oldest subscription library in Britain. It is not all past history, however, for in 1992 the world gold-panning championships were held here, with the Duke of Buccleugh (whose mid-19th century ancestors did much to improve miners' housing) waiving his mineral rights for the duration.

An 'adit' entrance to a lead mine, seen at the museum

The story of the Lowlands Covenanters and the extremes to which their religious enthusiasm took them is inseparably linked with Sir Walter Scott's *Old Mortality* (1816). The novel is based on anecdotes told by 'Old Mortality', a supporter of their cause who goes around cleaning up their tombs, and in particular tells the love story of the courageous young Covenanter, Morton, and Edith, grand-daughter of his Royalist opponent.

The village, set along the ridge of a hill, with the churchyard in the foreground

KILMARTIN

Strathclyde

28 MILES (45 KM) SOUTH OF OBAN

John Carswell is remembered now for printing a liturgy in Gaelic in 1567, but for many years after he died, it seems, it was his funeral day that folk recalled. So bad was the weather that his body could not be rowed across from Achnacloich to Ardchattan and thereafter a stormy day was reckoned to be as bad, or nearly as bad, as the day of Carswell's funeral.

Lying just inland from Lochs Crinan and Craignish on the Sound of Jura, the tiny grey village of Kilmartin is the focal point of an area studded with a galaxy of prehistoric sites. The sense of history in this still, quiet glen is all-pervading in its silence. Man has lived here since the dawn of history, probably arriving from across the sea, and over the ages has left a legacy that counts amongst the most inspiring and beautiful in all Scotland.

Just south of the village are the Nether Largie chambered cairns, the most notable of many in a 3 mile (5km), linear pre-Christian cemetery. The Neolithic South Cairn was used for probably over 1000 years for cremated and uncremated bodies. The

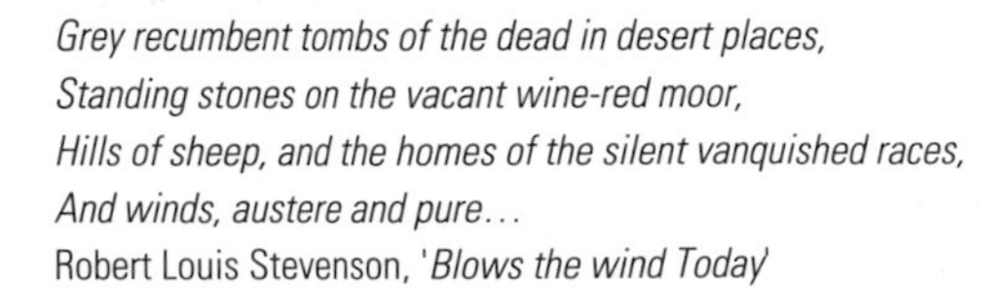

Grey recumbent tombs of the dead in desert places,
Standing stones on the vacant wine-red moor,
Hills of sheep, and the homes of the silent vanquished races,
And winds, austere and pure...
Robert Louis Stevenson, '*Blows the wind Today*'

Templewood stone circle

North Cairn is of Bronze Age date and has carved axe-head and cup-and-ring markings. Linear burial sites, found not uncommonly in Wessex, are rare in Scotland, and the carvings of bronze axes found on some of the tombs in this area are otherwise known only at Stonehenge, indicative of close links between Argyll and Wessex. Just west of the South Cairn is the Templewood circle of standing stones. A little further south, rising out of flat land beside the River Add, is the rock on which was built the prehistoric fortress of Dunadd, one of the 6th-century capitals of Dalriada from which the Celtic kingdom of Scotland was created. Near the top are three most poignant carvings in the rock, a man's footprint, a delicate drawing of a boar, and a basin. We can only guess that Scotland's earliest kings washed in the basin and stood in the footprint at their investiture ceremony.

The richness of Celtic art is most beautifully represented in the churchyard at Kilmartin, where there are two famous early Christian crosses. One is finely decorated with plaiting, the other carved with Christ crucified on one side, in Majesty on the other. Also in the graveyard are some splendid, recumbent medieval gravestones, of Malcolms of Poltalloch and Campbells of Duntrune. Richly sculptured and deeply cut, some show knights in armour.

In the village are the ruins of a 16th-century castle, while a little north the remains of Carnasserie Castle overlook the valley. This was also built in the 16th century, by John Carswell, first Protestant Bishop of the Isles – he who printed Knox's liturgy in Gaelic. The ruin still stands five storeys high, with kitchens on the ground floor and a room off the hall on the first floor in which is a finely ornamented fireplace. The views over the glen are beautiful.

Robert Owen was an influential social reformer but some of his ideas failed, notably his 'villages of co-operation', in which each person was to work for the good of the whole, and his Grand National Consolidated Trades Union. He himself recognised that much of his thinking was too advanced. On his deathbed in 1858, he said: 'I gave important truths to the world, and it was only for want of understanding that they were disregarded. I have been ahead of my time.'

NEW LANARK

Strathclyde

1 MILE (1.5 KM) SOUTH OF LANARK

New Lanark is the most outstanding factory village in Scotland, much of it recently and splendidly restored and revitalised as both a commercial visitor attraction and a living community. In 1784 David Dale and Richard Arkwright chose this narrow, wooded gorge to build new cotton-spinning mills, harnessing the waters of the Falls of Clyde to power their machinery. Initially Dale built four mills and then in 1789 added the 'New Buildings', a four-storeyed block with a bell-tower. He built blocks of tenement housing for the workers, strung along the hillside, and provided them with a church and a workers' institute.

In 1800 the Welshman Robert Owen, Dale's son-in-law, became owner-manager and it is his name that is now most closely associated with New Lanark. Owen introduced radically innovative reforms to the factory working conditions. He reduced working hours and did not allow children to work in the factory until they were ten. In the Institute for the Formation of Character he set up the world's first infant school, and in 1817 built a school for children aged

Below and opposite: the sandstone factory-workers' homes, built to house eight families each

three to ten. He built the Nursery Buildings to care for the orphan apprentices he found working there. When their contracts expired, the building was used for village housing. He started a scheme for old age pensioners. He improved housing and living conditions: 'I arranged superior stores and shops from which to supply every article of food, clothing etc., which they required...I had the whole of these articles of the best qualities supplied to the people at cost prices...The effect soon became visible in their improved health and superior dress, and the general comfort of their houses.' His philosophy was vindicated by increased output and higher profits, and he persuaded Parliament to incorporate some of his ideas in the Factory Act (1819). New Lanark today is his splendid memorial.

The mills closed in 1968 and by the time the Conservation Trust started work in 1974 the population of the village had fallen to about 80. Today it is about double that, with people living in the austere, but somehow not forbidding, tenement houses and in flats in the New Buildings. Many of the properties are owned by a housing association. Three of the mills still stand. In No 3 there is a Visitor Centre, reached through the Institute; in No 2 there is a large Edinburgh Woollen Mill shop, and plans for another visitor attraction are under way; No 1 is still derelict and awaits funding. Owen's 1813 Village Store, a forerunner of the Co-operative Movement, is now open to visitors as an 1820s shop and a 1920s shop, while the church is a community hall for the New Lanark villagers.

Corra Linn

Footpaths lead from the village into a nature reserve and along the wooded banks of the river to Corra Linn, the most famous of the Falls of Clyde and an inspiration to poets and painters including Wordsworth, Coleridge and Scott, Turner and Landseer. In 1708 a 'hall of mirrors' was built by the Corra Linn to give visitors the impression of being completely surrounded by water.

BRODICK CASTLE

Strathclyde

ISLE OF ARRAN

High above the Firth of Clyde, on the shores of the Isle of Arran, stands Brodick Castle. Backed by the magnificent peak of Goatfell, Brodick occupies a strong defensive position, guarding three routes to western Scotland, and the earliest record of a garden dates from 1710 when a wall was constructed around the present flower garden near to the castle.

However, the layout was overgrown with rhododendrons when the Duchess of Montrose arrived in the 1920s. In her plans to restore and extend the gardens, she was much helped by her son-in-law, Major J P T Boscawen, of Tresco Abbey. Many of the trees and plants came from Tresco, and also from the second generation of plant-hunters like Kingdon-Ward and the great George Forrest who brought back seemingly tender plants from the Himalayas and China which now flourish in the warmth of the Gulf Stream climate of Arran. Today, these magnificent gardens are cared for most skilfully by the National Trust for Scotland.

Left, parts of Brodick are medieval, but the castle was redesigned and rebuilt in the 17th century, and again in 1844

Above, the sundial is surrounded by orderly beds of annuals

Right, a spectacular shower of lilies

Surrounding the castle are spacious lawns edged by colourful beds containing a wide variety of shrubs, including the tall *Eucryphia* 'Nymansay', *Acer* campbellii, olearias and a group of modern hybrid azaleas. A door in the Flower Garden wall leads into a protected enclosure where *Cordyline banksii* and *Ceanothus arboreus* 'Trewithen Blue' flourish, as do acacias, gazanias, fuschias and diascias. In recent years, ribbon-bedding in four long borders has introduced dramatic colour during the summer.

Further down the sloping garden you come to the Pond Garden where plants as diverse in size as gunneras and dwarf primulas thrive. Magnolias and rhododendrons show boldly in spring, while *Crinodendron hookerianum* has pink lantern flowers in summer, and eucryphias and the fragrant lily-of-the-valley tree are at their best in August. The Woodland Garden is planted with rhododendrons and allied shrubs, including many that came from the Isle of Gigha as the gift of the late Sir James Horlick. There are magnolias which produce the most wonderful display of pink flowers on bare branches in April, and a fine *R. sinogrande*. But perhaps the greatest treasure of Brodick is the amazing size of the rhododendron blooms, some of them up to 2ft (0.6m) across.

Open daily. Tel: 01770 302202.

Left, a long view of the castle, across lawns framed with colourful beds

BOTHWELL CASTLE

Strathclyde

BOTHWELL, 7½ MILES (12 KM) SOUTH-EAST OF GLASGOW

On 29 August 1301, 30 wagons began a cumbersome two-day journey from Glasgow to the mighty fortress at Bothwell. Carried on these wagons were the parts for an enormous siege tower that had been commissioned by Edward I, the 'Hammer of the Scots', from the men of Glasgow. When the siege tower, or 'bellfry' as contemporary accounts call it, was reconstructed from its many sections, it stood higher than the castle walls. It was basically a vast platform on wheels, with a drawbridge at the top, that could be pushed close to the walls so that besiegers could storm the castle. Faced with this weapon, Bothwell fell to Edward's army within just a few days.

Bothwell Castle was one of the most important military strongholds in Scotland. Its great tower was built in the 1270s, and was a powerful structure with walls 80 feet (24 m) high and 15 feet (4.6 m) thick. Later, thick walls and a powerful gatehouse were added.

Because Bothwell was so prominent in the Scottish struggle for independence, it was attacked and fell many times during the 13th and 14th centuries. Each time damage was done and repairs were made, and so it can be difficult to date some of the surviving ruins. Several great towers and walls still jut defiantly into the air, giving the derelict castle an undeniable air of power.

Open all year, daily except winter Fridays, Christmas and New Year. Tel: 0131 668 8800.

Parts of Bothwell have survived since the 13th century

The old ruined castle occupies a secure site on Loch Awe

INNIS CONNEL CASTLE

Strathclyde

LOCH AWE, 18 MILES (29 KM) EAST OF OBAN

In the 15th century Donald, the infant heir to the Lord of the Isles, was brought to the island fortress of Innis Connel as a prisoner by the Campbell clan. By the time he managed to escape, Donald had reached adulthood. He did not enjoy his freedom for long, for he was recaptured after an ill-conceived invasion of Badenoch in 1503, and was taken to Edinburgh. Poor Donald remained a prisoner at Edinburgh for 40 years.

Innis Connel was an important stronghold of the Campbells of Argyll and was one of their earliest castles. Local tradition suggests that the castle dates from the 11th century, along with the founders of the great Campbell clan, although there is no architectural evidence that it is so old.

The present building, a squat, square tower, draped in ivy and nestling amid trees, probably dates from the 13th century, and was enlarged in the 15th century. The alterations changed the castle from a simple rectangular tower to a strong enclosure with thick walls following the shape of the island, complete with additional towers. Innis Connel still occupies its little island in Loch Awe, although the view of the castle from the road is somewhat obscured by trees, especially in summer.

The island is privately owned, and there is no public access.

The monument to Nelson, erected immediately after the battle of Trafalgar, 37 years before the column in London's Trafalgar Square

TAYNUILT
Strathclyde

9 MILES (14.5 KM) EAST OF OBAN

On a grassy hillock overlooking the village, near the parish church, is a 12ft (3.5m) high granite pillar that is the earliest monument to Nelson in Britain. Something of a surprise in a West Highland village, particularly as, at the start of the 19th century, there was more sympathy in these parts for the Auld Alliance with France than for the 1707 Act of Union with England. The explanation lies in the old furnace works that can be visited on the shore of Loch Etive. Banned from tree-felling in England, iron-smelters moved their furnaces to Scotland and in 1753 a company in Cumbria established a furnace at Taynuilt, which, being heavily forested in oak and beech, was well able to supply the necessary charcoal. Iron ore was brought up from Ulverston to Kelly's Pier and some 600 men, many from Lancashire, were employed in the manufacture of pig iron. Most of the village's granite houses date from this period. It was these furnacemen who in 1805 erected the monument to Nelson. In 1874 the 'bloomery' closed, put out of business by the introduction of blast furnaces, and the village became the quiet place it is today, a haunt of fishermen, nature-lovers and walkers who explore the beautiful countryside around about. Taynuilt is a stop on the magnificently scenic Glasgow-to-Oban line. Part of the station houses a brewery.

AYR

Strathclyde

12 MILES (19 KM) SOUTH-WEST OF KILMARNOCK

'Auld Ayr, wham ne'er a toun surpasses
For honest men and bonnie lasses.'
Robert Burns, *Tam o' Shanter* (1791)

The Burns Monument with its formal gardens, and the single-arched Brig o' Doon

The principal seaside resort on this stretch of coast – its broad, sandy beach is said to be the most heavily trodden in Scotland – Ayr has a past going far back beyond William Wallace's burning alive of English soldiers in their wooden barracks here in 1297. In medieval days, the town was Scotland's leading west coast harbour. By the 18th century it was trading across the Atlantic, and in the 19th it became a major industrial port. At the same time, as sea-bathing became fashionable, Ayr blossomed as a smart resort for the local gentry, whose town residences have been transformed into hotels and boarding houses. The attractive parks are a legacy of this period and, as the names of Troon and Turnberry suggest, this is prime golfing territory. Many visitors to Ayr are pilgrims on the trail of the poet Robert Burns. He was baptised in the 17th-century Auld Kirk, and he and his friends used to meet in an alehouse which is now the Tam o' Shanter Museum. The cottage where he was born in 1759 is on the southern outskirts of the town, with a museum of his manuscripts and personal belongings. Thomas Hamilton designed the nearby Burns Monument in graceful classical style in 1820.

CRARAE GARDENS

Strathclyde

MINARD, 10 MILES (16 KM) SOUTH OF INVERARAY

On the road that runs along the edge of Loch Fyne, north from Minard Castle towards Inveraray, is the wonderful glen garden of Crarae. Originally started by Grace Campbell in the early years of this century, Crarae was inspired in part by her great nephew, Reginald Farrer – the plant collector and traveller, who introduced into Britain a number of rhododendron species from his trips to Kansu in 1914 and to Upper Burma in 1919 – and perhaps also by Sir John Stirling Maxwell of Pollok. With her son, Sir George Campbell, she spent many years creating this 'Himalayan ravine' garden in a Highland glen. In 1978, Sir George's son, Sir Ilay, transferred the larger part of Crarae to a charitable trust, so that this remarkable garden would be preserved.

These magnificent gardens fill the glen

An unusual find in a country garden – Crarae has its own ancient chambered tomb

Above Crarae is Beinn Ghlas, and where the highest larches end you can see the natural scrub of oak, alder, hazel, birch and rowan that had to be cleared from the lower slopes when the garden was originally created. Beyond the lawns and the two large borders immediately around the Lodge, there are views over Loch Fyne, with, in spring, massed colour of azaleas and a splendid *Acer Tschonoskii*. Following the Crarae Burn further into the Upper Glen the dramatic colours of azaleas, set against a backdrop of decorative hardwoods, catch the eye. The shrub planting includes olearias and the New Zealand pittosporum, which grows strongly.

Close to the waterfall viewpoint there is a fine Japanese dogwood, *Cornus Kousa*, which turns in October to contrast dramatically with the red-leaved azaleas, witch hazel and with *Disanthus cercidifolius*. When you reach the top bridge, azaleas give colour to the foreground, and *Rhododendron davidsonianum* stands beyond with its tulle-like flowers ranging from pale pink to lilac-mauve. Among the hybrid rhododendrons that you can see at Crarae are *Loderi* 'King George', 'Dairymaid', Laura Aberconway' and 'Beauty of Littleworth'. Autumn colour is also quite remarkable, with sorbus, acers, liriodendrons, cotoneasters and berberis competing for attention. With the backdrop of waterfalls and the rushing Crarae Burn, this is indeed a garden of great beauty and individuality.

Open all year, daily. Tel: 01546 86614.

The railway's purpose was to take visitors arriving from Oban to Torosay Castle

MULL & WEST HIGHLAND NARROW GAUGE RAILWAY

Strathclyde

CRAIGNURE, ISLE OF MULL, NEAR FERRY LANDING FROM OBAN

Most miniature gauge railways are purely for fun, and often run in circuits. The man credited with their invention, Sir Arthur Heywood, envisaged them being useful for estate or military purposes, but he would have approved of the 10¼in (260mm) gauge Mull & West Highland Railway – Scotland's only island railway connects with the ferry from Oban to take passengers to one of the island's principal tourist attractions, the mid 19th-century Torosay Castle. The connections are generous, allowing passengers half an hour to find their land legs and saunter along the front.

The idea for the railway stemmed from the difficulty the castle's owners were having in persuading people to walk the 2 miles (3km) from the pier. A group of promoters was formed and surveying began. Part of the route uses an old carriage drive that was built in the 1850s between the castle and the pier but never used, because the Kirk refused to allow it to cross church land for the final part. It was so overgrown

with rhododendrons 120 years later that the survey had to be done on hands and knees, but the colours in early summer are now one of the railway's attractions.

In complete contrast to the secluded character of the carriage drive is the first section of the line, which enjoys spectacular views over the Sound of Mull to Ben Nevis, the Glencoe Hills and the Island of Lismore. A stop at a loop named Tarmstedt is an opportunity for passengers to watch the engine take water. Its naming after a German town is due to a former owner of Torosay, who was also the first chairman of the Mull & West Highland; he began two escape attempts from a German prison camp at that narrow gauge station – the second was successful.

Another curious link that the railway has is with the Puffing Billy Railway in Victoria, Australia. The search for a suitable prototype on which to base the Mull & West Highland's third locomotive ended with a set of plans of a tank engine used on the best-known tourist railway in the Antipodes. The result is now thought to be the largest tank engine of 10¼in (260mm) gauge in the world, which can haul 11 carriages with 190 passengers for the 20-minute journey.

Train service: during the Easter holiday, then daily from late April to mid October. Tel: 016802 494.

Getting Lady of the Isles *ready for action*

The village seen from Fionnphort harbour

IONA
Strathclyde

5-MINUTE PASSENGER FERRY FROM FIONNPHORT, ISLAND OF MULL

'That man is little to be envied whose…piety would not grow warmer among the ruins of Iona.' So wrote Samuel Johnson in 1775 in *A Journey to the Western Islands of Scotland.* Today, there are some who may find their piety grows warmer, and Iona's special atmosphere is better savoured away from that well-worn sightseers' trail between jetty and abbey, sitting quietly in the wild flowers up on a green hill or walking across the multi-coloured pebbles of a peaceful bay.

The houses of Iona village line the island's eastern shore, their grey gables full face to the ferry that daily brings another influx of pilgrims to this tiny cradle of Christianity. It was here, in AD 563, that St Columba arrived from Ireland to establish a monastery, a base for the missionary journeys that converted the Pictish heathens of the north to his Celtic Christianity. This became a place of holiness, a place of learning, a place of artistic excellence (where work began on *The Book of Kells*), a place of power. Between the 9th century and the Reformation some 48 Scottish kings were buried here, in Reilig Odhrain. Of Columba's monastery little remains, but it was rebuilt in the 11th century by Queen Margaret and her charming, pink granite Chapel of St Oran is the oldest building on the island. Near it is one of the 350 carved crosses that stood on Iona before the Reformation. Since the turn of the century the Church of Scotland and the Iona Community founded by Lord George MacLeod have carried out extensive restoration work on the abbey. Enjoy the jaunty medieval carvings on some of the piers. The 13th-century nunnery remains a flowery ruin. Otherwise there is just the village shop, a café, a couple of hotels, a craft shop, a second-hand bookshop and a tea-room in the abbey.

CRINAN
Strathclyde

6 MILES (9.5 KM) NORTH-WEST OF LOCHGILPHEAD

Crinan is a tiny place at the foot of a wooded rocky promontory beside Loch Crinan. It is also at the western end of the Crinan Canal, and it is this that brings it to life. For yachtsmen it is the gate that opens on to the seas of the Hebrides, and its locks and basin are always busy with the clicking of mainstays and the squeaking and rubbing of fenders. There was little here except a 7th-century church until work started in 1793 on the canal that was to run 9 miles (14.5km) east to Ardrishaig, linking the Sound of Jura with Loch Fyne. This would save ships the slow and hazardous journey around the Mull of Kintyre and speed up deliveries of fish to Glasgow. John Rennie was the chief engineer for the project, which was beset with difficulties from the start. Finances proved a problem, at one point the canal banks collapsed, and what with one thing and another it did not open to traffic until 1809. Even then Thomas Telford had to be called in to make improvements and work continued until 1817. The canal has never been a commercial success but the basin at Crinan today is a popular marina and an attractive setting for the handful of houses and the hotel that has stood here since the 1890s.

A Royal Progress

In 1847 Queen Victoria travelled along the Crinan Canal on her way from Glasgow to Oban, a route which was to be marketed by the ferry company MacBrayne's as the 'Royal Route'. The Royal Route (and, of course, MacBrayne's) feature in Neil Munro's irresistibly comic tales of Para Handy and his 'puffer' boat *Vital Spark*, mostly set in and around Loch Fyne in the first two decades of the 20th century.

The Crinan Hotel, overlooking the locks that open on to the sea

KILCHURN CASTLE

Strathclyde

18 MILES (29 KM) EAST OF OBAN

In an area of reeds and marshes at the northern end of Loch Awe stands Kilchurn Castle, its granite walls and chimneys rising like jagged teeth above the trees. Its position on a peninsula reaching out into the loch gave it some protection from attack on three sides.

The beauty of Kilchurn's setting on this attractive loch has attracted many an artist, but on closer inspection, time has not dealt kindly with the little lakeside fortress and only a shell remains to be seen. Until recently, Kilchurn's unstable walls were a danger to visitors, but these have been secured and the castle may now be viewed from the grounds.

Kilchurn Castle began as a simple square tower with five floors. It was raised in the 15th century by Colin Campbell, 1st Earl of Breadalbane. In the 16th and 17th centuries, the castle was extended. The square tower was incorporated into a small courtyard, with three corner towers, forming an irregular quadrangle. Oddly, the only way into the castle seems to have been through the main door of the keep and across its ground floor. Gun loops placed at regular intervals all around the walls suggest that Kilchurn's builders were more concerned with repelling sudden attacks by Highlanders than in resisting lengthy sieges.

Open access at any reasonable time. Tel: 0131 668 8800.

Kilchurn's walls, close to toppling over, have recently been strengthened

Culzean is superbly set on a cliff top, with beautiful terraced gardens on the landward side

CULZEAN CASTLE

Strathclyde

4 MILES (6.5 KM) WEST OF MAYBOLE

Where once the medieval tower-house of the chiefs of the Clan Kennedy perched on its cliff-top, looking out towards Arran and Kintyre, there now stands one of 18th-century architect Robert Adam's finest works.

The great mansion was built during the 1770s for the 10th Earl of Cassillis, chief of the Kennedys, and remained in their family until it was given to the National Trust for Scotland in 1945. Since that time much restoration work has been carried out and the splendid state rooms once again show off the magnificent decorative plasterwork in the original colours specified in Adam's designs. The most notable features of the Culzean interiors are the oval staircase and the unusual circular drawing room with its specially woven carpet. The west wing of the castle dates from 1879, when the 14th Earl needed more space for his large family.

Culzean Castle also contains the National Guest Flat, an apartment which was given, after World War II, to US President Eisenhower for use during his lifetime. There is now an exhibition relating to Eisenhower's links with the castle.

As well as its beautiful gardens, the Culzean estate includes Scotland's first country park, established in 1969 and centred on the buildings of the former Home Farm.

Open from April to October daily. Tel: 016556 274.

CASTLE STALKER

Strathclyde

18 MILES (29 KM) NORTH OF OBAN

Standing on a tiny island in Loch Laich, this small tower house can be seen from the road that runs from Ballachulish towards Oban. It bears some resemblance to the castle of Eilean Donan, since both are set in lonely sites, surrounded by water, and are simple tower structures.

Historically, it would appear that access to Castle Stalker has always been by boat, and no causeway has ever been built to make it more easily accessible, but at low tide it is possible to wade across the shallow waters of the loch.

The castle itself is a rectangular tower, about 45 feet (14m) by 36 feet (11m) at its base, and was built in the 16th century. The fact that its walls were nine feet (2.7m) thick, coupled with the inaccessibility of its site, meant that it was fairly well protected against would-be invaders. The entrance was at first floor level, and access originally would have been up wooden steps, or a ladder that could have been drawn up into the tower in times of danger. The stone stairway that can be seen today was a later addition.

Castle Stalker became derelict after the Second Jacobite Rising in the 18th century, and was restored only recently.

The castle is not open to the public, but clearly visible from the main road.

Cut off from the land, Castle Stalker's defences were effective throughout its history

One of Scotland's four Royal palaces, Linlithgow was built for James I of Scotland

LINLITHGOW PALACE

Lothian

7 MILES (11.5 KM) SOUTH OF GRANGEMOUTH

Rising dramatically from the shores of Linlithgow Loch is a great square palace-fortress, which dates from the 15th century. Although there was a fortified residence here as early as the mid 12th century, and Edward I built a manor here in 1302, it was not until 1425 that work began on the castle that may be seen today.

The Scottish King, James I, gave orders that a royal residence should be constructed on the site of the earlier buildings, and although Linlithgow was primarily a palace, the architect incorporated a number of defensive features. There was a drawbridge and a barbican, and the walls of the four corner towers were immensely thick. The windows in the lower floors were protected by iron bars, the holes for which can still be seen in the stone. Around the early 1500s, machicolations were added.

Linlithgow has played its part in Scotland's history. Mary, Queen of Scots was born here in 1542, Charles I slept here in 1633 and Cromwell stayed in the Palace in the winter of 1650–51. When the Duke of Cumberland's army bivouacked in Linlithgow in 1746 *en route* to their encounter with Prince Charles Edward Stuart's army at Culloden Moor, fires were left burning which gutted this handsome building.

Open all year, daily except Christmas and New Year. Tel: 0131 668 8800.

Cromwell bombarded the castle for three months in 1650, and it came under heavy attack by the forces of William of Orange in 1689.

EDINBURGH CASTLE

Lothian

EDINBURGH

There was no capital city of Scotland, as such, until the end of the Middle Ages. Before that, Scotland's capital was wherever the king and his court happened to be. But the magnificent fortress squatting firmly on its plug of rock was a great favourite with Scottish kings, and has played a vital role in history on many occasions. It changed hands several times when the Scots were fighting for independence from England under Robert the Bruce, and became a royal residence under the Stuart kings.

Today, it is a museum – it houses the Scottish National War Memorial and the Scottish crown jewels – and is the venue for the spectacular annual Edinburgh Military Tattoo. It still dominates the ancient city from its rocky pinnacle, and even though it has been battered and bruised through the centuries, remains one of the most impressive and best-known castles in the world.

The origins of Edinburgh Castle are shrouded in mystery. Although the great rock on which the castle stands would probably have attracted earlier strongholds, there is no archaeological evidence to prove the site was used earlier than the 11th century. Malcolm III, before his death in 1093, raised a wooden fortress here and his son, David I, built a church to the memory of his mother in the 1120s. This tiny chapel is the oldest surviving building in the castle. Thereafter, Edinburgh became an important gamepiece in the struggles between Edward I and

Below and right, Edinburgh Castle, at the heart of this great city, is one of the most famous in the world

Robert the Bruce in the late 13th century. Edward seized it in 1296, bombarding it with huge boulders from his great war machines. The garrison surrendered after only eight days, and Edward installed 350 of his own soldiers to hold it securely.

In 1313 the Earl of Moray, acting for Bruce, scaled the daunting cliffs with only 30 men and routed the English. Bruce then ordered that the castle be utterly destroyed, so that it could never again be used by Edward's forces. He underestimated Edward's tenacity, for a few years later Edward retook the site, and set about repairing the damage, even planting gardens and orchards in anticipation of a lengthy stay. But the Scots were undeterred, and in 1341 a small party of Scottish soldiers disguised themselves as merchants and quickly ambushed the startled garrison.

The vast sprawl of the castle contains buildings from many centuries. The fine half-moon battery and portcullis gate date from the 1570s, while the splendid Great Hall and the handsome palace were built for James IV in the early 16th century.

Open all year, daily. Tel: 0131 668 8800.

HOPETOUN HOUSE

Lothian

2 MILES (3 KM) WEST OF SOUTH QUEENSFERRY

A swathe of grassy parkland cuts through the wooded southern shore of the Firth of Forth and at its centre stands one of Scotland's most splendid mansions, Hopetoun House, the home of the Marquess of Linlithgow. Begun in 1699, it is the creation of two of Scotland's most celebrated architects – Sir William Bruce, who was responsible for the original building, and William Adam, who enlarged it some time later.

The Marquess's ancestors, the Hope family, were diligent in their public service and in their studies of the law and the sciences. In the 17th century Sir Thomas Hope rose to become Charles I's King's Advocate, and his sons followed him into the legal profession. It was his grandson, John Hope, who purchased the land on which Hopetoun House now stands.

Hopetoun's interiors are a sumptuous progression of richly decorated rooms which provide a suitably grand setting for the fine works of art, including notable paintings by such artists as Canaletto, Gainsborough and Raeburn, displayed within them. The red drawing room, with its scarlet damask

The sweeping front of the house, below, and right, richly damasked walls offset Old Masters

wall covering and intricate gilded plaster ceiling, is one of the most magnificent rococo rooms in Scotland, while the gold state dining room is a set piece of the Regency period. Hot food would have been brought here from the kitchen in a steam-heated container, pushed along a railway track, then raised in a lift to a warming oven from where it was served by the butler and footmen. This is also where the family portraits are congregated.

The front stairs are an important feature of the original house and are in complete contrast with the state apartments, having mellow pine panelling with painted panels and borders which are beautifully carved with flowers, fruit, corn stalks and peapods.

One unusual attraction at Hopetoun House is the roof-top viewing platform. The wonderful panorama over the surrounding grounds to the countryside beyond and, of course, the Forth, with its famous bridges away to the east, is well worth the climb.

Hopetoun also has a number of special exhibitions, including a family museum and 'The Building of Hopetoun', commemorating the architects and craftspeople whose talents combined to create this magnificent building. The contracts and accounts make fascinating reading. Out in the tack room off the courtyard is a display, entitled 'Horse and Man in Lowland Scotland', devoted to the role played by the horse in the economic and social life of the area before the motor vehicle took over.

Open from mid-April to early October daily. Tel: 0131 331 2451.

When King George IV came to Hopetoun in 1822 the ceremonials were masterminded by Sir Walter Scott. With the 4th Earl of Hopetoun as their Captain-General, a company of gentlemen archers formed a guard of honour for the King's arrival. He was so impressed that the company were granted the title of 'King's Bodyguard in Scotland' – a ceremonial role which continues to this day.

HOUSE OF THE BINNS

Lothian

BLACKNESS, 4 MILES (6.5 KM) EAST OF LINLITHGOW

Two years of major structural restoration works have recently been completed at this fascinating house, predominantly a Regency mansion but also displaying the changing architectural tastes which have taken place here from 1612 onwards. It has evolved from a tall, grey, three-storeyed building with small windows and twin turrets into a pretty U-shaped house with crenellations and embellished windows. Inside, it has some beautiful early 17th-century moulded plaster ceilings.

Before coming into the care of the National Trust for Scotland, the House of The Binns had been the home of the Dalyell family since 1612. One of its most colourful characters was General Tam Dalyell, an ardent Royalist who was captured by Cromwell's army at the Battle of Worcester but escaped from the Tower of London and fled to Russia, where he organised the Tzar's army. He was recalled at the Restoration to command Charles II's forces in Scotland, and was the founder of the Royal Scots Greys in 1681. His boots and comb can still be seen in the house, together with a thimble belonging to his grand-daughter, Magdalen (who made a 'set of hingings for the whole hoose') and the drawings of Sir John Graham Dalyell, who taught Darwin.

Open June to September every afternoon, except Friday. Tel: 01506 834255.

A large pier-glass apparently doubles the size of this comfortable room

Antique furniture,collected at the turn of the century, adorns the house

LAURISTON CASTLE

Lothian

1 MILE (1.5 KM) EAST OF CRAMOND

A particular nightmare of school days for some of us can be directly attributed to Lauriston Castle, for it was John Napier, the son of its first owner, who invented logarithms! The house, set in 30 acres (12ha) of lovely parkland and peaceful gardens, has considerably more charm for most people than the mathematics, however.

A number of notable Scots have called it home over the years, including the 18th-century financier, John Law, who held high office at the Court of pre-revolution France, and William Robert Reid, proprietor of a prestigious firm of cabinet-makers in Edinburgh. The latter was an enthusiastic collector of antiques, fine furniture, prints and other works of art, and he bought Lauriston Castle in 1902 to provide a suitable setting for his collections. In order to preserve their cherished home and its contents intact, Mr and Mrs Reid bequeathed the entire property to the nation in 1926.

The oldest part of the house, a tower-house which now forms the south-west corner of the building, dates back to the late 16th century and includes the lovely Oak Room; the remainder was added in two phases during the 19th century.

Open from April to October daily, except Friday; weekends only in winter. Tel: 0131 336 2060.

A concealed stairway leads from one corner of the Oak Room to a small chamber in the tower wall. It may have been used as a hideaway, but a spy-hole, blocked when a new ceiling was added in 1827, suggests a more sinister purpose.

The one-oared ferry boat and the ferryman's house, on the far side of the Almond

CRAMOND

Lothian

IN THE NORTH-WESTERN OUTSKIRTS OF EDINBURGH

The minutes of the local Kirk Session make surprisingly scurrilous reading. Those dated 5 August 1660 record that: *Margrat Corstoune...gave in a bill of slander against Isbell Wallace...quhairin was conteind that the said Isbell Wallace had said that the said Margrat was a witch or that shee had the carriage of a witch, and a runnagate, and blackned bitch. The said Isbell gave in a bill against Margrat Corstoune quhairin was conteind that the said Margrat had cald her a drunken harlot and lowne.*

Cramond today is a charming place of old white-painted stone cottages that layer steeply down to an ancient quay at the mouth of the River Almond. A ferry boat takes passengers across the narrow estuary to Lord Rosebery's Dalmeny estates. A wooded riverside walk leads past a small boat park to a weir and a ruined mill. A picture postcard image, perhaps, but one that belies its past. On the orders of Emperor Antoninus Pius, around AD142 the Romans built a harbour and fort here, at the eastern end of the Empire's northernmost frontier line. Part of the fort can be seen near the church, a mainly 17th-century building on a site used for many, many centuries before that. Note its fine carved gravestones. Near by are Cramond Tower, a medieval defensive tower, and Cramond House, home of successive lairds of Cramond. Below it, in the 18th and 19th centuries, the waters of the Almond powered no less than five mills. Originally used for corn and cloth, by 1752 they were manufacturing iron nails, spades, hoops, cart axles and so on. Cockle Mill, closest to the quay where iron was imported and finished products exported, is now a private house. The old workers' cottages have been renovated, while the main forge, Fairafar Mill, is the ruin that stands by the weir – silent testimony to noisier, dirtier days.

DIRLETON CASTLE

Lothian

DIRLETON, 11 MILES (17.5 KM) NORTH-EAST OF EDINBURGH

This sturdy castle was raised in the 13th century, probably on the remains of an earlier fortress. The principal building was the impressive three-storeyed round keep or 'drum' tower, supported by a complex arrangement of other towers and walls. In the 14th and 15th centuries the castle was considerably enlarged, to include a chapel with a prison beneath, and a pit-prison hewn from the rock below that. Although a ruin, Dirleton still presents an imposing face to the world and crossing the modern wooden footbridge to the great gatehouse, it is easy to appreciate the difficulties faced by any would-be attacker.

Dorothea, wife of the rebellious Earl of Gowrie, was probably one of the saddest residents of Dirleton Castle. Her husband was executed in 1585 after a plot to seize Stirling Castle was discovered, and all his lands and castles were taken by King James VI, leaving Dorothea and her 15 children poverty-stricken. The king granted Dirleton Castle to Gowrie's great rival, the Earl of Arran, who kept it until the castle and its lands were restored to Dorothea almost two years later. Then, in 1600, two of her sons were involved in the mysterious 'Gowrie Conspiracy', when it was alleged that they tried to kill the King. Although the maiming of the corpses of Dorothea's sons was very public, details of the entire affair remained secret.

Open all year daily, except Christmas and New Year. Tel: 0131 668 8800.

Dirleton is built on a rock outcrop, surrounded by the remains of a moat

PLANTS FROM THE PAST

Lothian

BELHAVEN, DUNBAR

Within a mile of the North Sea coast in Scotland is one of the more remarkable country gardens, Plants from the Past, situated in North Street, Belhaven. During the past five years, Dr David Stuart and James Sutherland have restored a walled kitchen garden and replanted it to a mid-18th-century design, so that, to turn from the narrow village streets through the gates and into a fine parterre is like taking a step back in time. The plant conservationist will also be delighted, however, as the two owners are not interested in modern cultivars, but rather in older forms of herbaceous plants.

Totally derelict when it was found, the site is surrounded by lovely sandstone walls and slopes gently towards the beach. On the higher ground, the owners found an early 18th-century building that seemed to have been used as an apple store, and boasted a tiny fireplace in the upstairs room, and this charming structure, now restored, serves as the office. From the upper windows, the parterre, which follows that planted at Yester House in the 1750s, seems to consist of a maze of gravel paths separating colourful beds, while at one side of the layout a raised grass walkway leads through to the nursery.

With a determined effort to recreate the planting of the correct date, the owners have placed mandrakes next to the lovely *Primula vulgaris subsp. Sibthorpii*, and 'Giant White' lavender alongside *Artemisia pontica*. Above these plants are Persian lilac, *Eleagnus augustifolia* and many old roses from 'Pompon de Bourgogne' to 'Maiden's Blush' and 'Quatre Saisons'.

Herbs, too, are historically accurate, with a cornel bush and a myrobalan, as well as sorrels, tarragon and tree onions. Plymouth strawberries, their seeds on the surface of the fruit turned into little points, are to be found, together with flamed pinks, double buttercups and soapworts, a pretty double form of the greater celandine, and tulips that range from 'Keizerskroon' to *Tulipa clusiana*. At Plants from the Past, the visitor can enjoy the dramatic colours, subtle textures and the half-remembered scents of old varieties secure in the knowledge that each purchase they make will help preserve the future for some of these rare plants.

Open from March to September, most days. Tel: 0368 63223.

Left and below, Plants from the Past cultivates a splendid collection of older varieties

Below and right, Tantallon, with its towering red sandstone walls poised on the edge of the cliffs, is a spectacular sight

TANTALLON CASTLE

Lothian

2½ MILES (4 KM) EAST OF NORTH BERWICK

To enable Tantallon to withstand sieges, arrangements were made for the castle to take in supplies from the seaward side. The remains of a crane bastion can be seen, where provisions were winched from boats anchored below, and it is likely that there was another one in the now ruined sea gate.

The great red walls of Tantallon Castle form one of the strongest and most daunting castles in Scotland. Perched on a spur of rock, with sheer cliffs plummeting into frothing seas on three of its sides, the fourth side is protected by a formidable array of ditches and walls. Rising from one of the three great gaping ditches, and sweeping clear across the neck of the promontory, is a vast curtain of red sandstone. This wall is 12 feet (3.7m) thick, and a staggering 50 feet (15m) tall. Although cannons and storms have battered this mighty wall, it remains one of the most impressive defensive features of any castle in Britain.

Tantallon is associated with one of Scotland's most famous families – the Red Douglases, Earls of Angus. It came into their hands at the end of the 14th century, and became their base as they plotted and fought against their enemies. But it was not until 1528 that the mighty fortress of Tantallon was seriously put to the test, when King James V himself laid siege to the Red Douglas stronghold.

Sixteenth-century Scottish politics were complicated, but, essentially, Archibald Douglas, 6th Earl of Angus, had kept the young James V a virtual prisoner in Edinburgh during his minority. James finally managed to escape, and once he was old enough to act for himself, he charged Douglas with treason. James brought a great battery of guns from Dunbar Castle, and for 20 days pounded the walls of Tantallon with everything he had. Tantallon, however, stood firm – perhaps because the great ditches to the front of the castle prevented the guns from being brought too close, and perhaps because the king ran short of powder and shot. The castle eventually fell to James, but as a result of negotiations rather than firepower. Douglas fled the country, and James began work to reinforce and repair Tantallon's medieval defences. After the King's death, Douglas returned from exile in 1543 and immediately began plotting against the Regent of Scotland, the Earl of Arran.

The ruins at Tantallon are impressive and the Mid Tower, which has been changed and developed through the centuries, stands almost complete. It was originally five storeys, but suffered during the 1528 siege. In 1556, a Fore Tower was added, designed both to withstand and to house cannon. The East Tower was also five storeys, and there are still stairs in the massive curtain wall that lead to the battlements.

Open April to September daily, and most days in winter. Tel: 0131 668 8800.

CRAIGMILLAR CASTLE

Lothian

2½ MILES (4 KM) SOUTH-EAST OF EDINBURGH

Buildings from four different periods make up the splendid ruins at Craigmillar. A simple L-plan tower house was built here in the late 14th century, of red-grey sandstone. In the 1420s, this sturdy tower was fortified by the addition of a 28 foot (8.5 m) wall with round towers at the corners, which ran all the way around it. Another set of walls and other buildings were added in the 16th and 17th centuries, including a chapel and kitchens, the remains of which can still be seen.

Although Craigmillar is a good example of a late medieval fortress, it is perhaps better known for its role in history. The first significant bloody act at Craigmillar was the murder of the Earl of Mar by a jealous brother in 1477. It was attacked and seriously damaged by the Earl of Hereford for Henry VIII in 1544, but was sufficiently repaired for Mary, Queen of Scots to retreat there following the murder of a favourite secretary in 1566. While Mary grieved for her loss, her noblemen plotted revenge. It is not known whether Mary was a party to the plot, but a pact was signed that resulted in the murder of Mary's estranged husband, Lord Darnley. While convalescing from a disease, his house was blown up. When his body was recovered, it was found that Darnley had been strangled before the explosion.

Open all year daily except winter Fridays. Tel: 0131 668 8800.

Craigmillar is linked to a notorious incident in the life of Mary, Queen of Scots

The jagged ruins of St Andrews Castle cling to a low grassy cliff on the coast

ST ANDREWS CASTLE

Fife

ST ANDREWS, 13 MILES (21 KM) SOUTH-EAST OF DUNDEE

In March 1546 the Protestant preacher George Wishart was burned in front of the walls of St Andrews Castle by the ambitious Archbishop of St Andrews, Cardinal David Beaton. Beaton was not a popular man, chiefly because he refused to agree to the marriage of Henry VIII's Protestant son to the Scottish king's Catholic daughter. Later that year, a group of Protestant Fife lairds gained access to the castle and murdered Beaton, hanging his body from the castle walls in a pair of sheets. Following this, a long siege began, as the forces of the Regent of Scotland tried to oust them from the castle.

It was during this turbulent time that the famous mine and counter-mine were dug. The attackers' mine was intended to go under the foundations, so that the wall would weaken, while the counter-mine attempted to stop it. You can still walk through these two tunnels, which give a unique insight into medieval warfare.

This ancient castle was built and used by the Bishops and Archbishops of St Andrews. It comprises a five-sided enclosure, protected on two sides by the sea, with buildings dating from the 12th to the 16th centuries that served as palace, fortress, and prison.

Open all year daily, except Christmas and New Year. Tel: 0131 668 8800.

One of the castle's most famous features is its sinister bottle dungeon. This is a pit 24 feet (7.3m) deep, which is narrow at the top and wider at the bottom – much like the shape of a bottle. Once you are inside, you cannot scale the walls to escape. Hewn out of solid rock, it has no windows or openings for air.

LOWER LARGO

Fife

2 MILES (3 KM) NORTH-EAST OF LEVEN

The original of one of fiction's most famous characters was born at Lower Largo in 1676. Alexander Selkirk was a shoemaker's son. In 1695 he was summoned to answer for `indecent behaviour' in church, but he had already run away to sea. Serving on various expeditions in the Pacific, in 1704 he was marooned on Juan Fernandez Island after quarrelling with his captain. He survived there alone for more than four years until a passing English ship rescued him, and his story of his adventures inspired Daniel Defoe's *Robinson Crusoe*. Selkirk died in 1721, and a statue of him in his goatskins adorns the cottage in which he was born. Lower Largo was once a fishing port on Largo Bay, but the last fishing boat was sold in the 1940s and the village is now a retirement colony and holiday resort, with a sandy beach and golf links. Upper Largo, inland, has the church where Alexander Selkirk's parents are buried. Sir Andrew Wood, who led two Scottish ships to a notable triumph over five English vessels off Dunbar in 1498, is also buried there. He had a canal built from his house to the church and liked to be rowed to services in his eight-oared barge.

Looking for a rescue: the statue of Alexander Selkirk was erected in 1885

A masterpiece of Edwardian elegance in the best Scottish traditions

HILL OF TARVIT

Fife

2½ MILES (4 KM) SOUTH OF CUPAR

When F B Sharp bought the modest house standing on this site at around the turn of the century, then known as Wemyss Hall, he very soon set about creating for himself a much larger house in which to display the considerable collections he had built up. That is not to say that the house was entirely unsuitable. Indeed, in one respect it was the perfect showcase for the beautiful French furniture – it had been designed by Sir William Bruce, a noted Scottish architect who was much influenced by French style.

The house simply wasn't large enough for the extensive belongings of Mr Sharp, which included fine antiques, Flemish tapestries, paintings and Chinese porcelain. He chose Sir Robert Lorimer as his architect and decided to simply fill in the space between the two existing wings.

Each of the new rooms created here was designed specifically to suit their contents, and today they display not only Sharp's splendid antiques, but also illustrate the imaginative skill of the architect and the excellent taste of his employer.

As well as all this, visitors to Hill of Tarvit today can gain an insight into the workings of such a mansion in Edwardian times, notably in the restored laundry. Concerts and art exhibitions are regularly held here.

Open over Easter, then from May to October daily. Tel: 01334 53127.

CULROSS
Fife

7 MILES (11 KM) WEST OF DUNFERMLINE

In the 16th and 17th centuries Culross was one of the largest ports in Scotland with a flourishing trade across the North Sea in local salt and coal. The Industrial Revolution dealt a blow to the economy, the royal burgh of Culross became a backwater, and its narrow, steep, cobbled streets stood still. By careful restoration work, the National Trust for Scotland has created a showpiece here, a treasure trove of 16th-century burgh architecture that looks much as it must have done in its heyday. George Bruce, a coal merchant who played a leading role in Culross's development, in 1597 built himself The Palace. It is a splendid example of a grand town house, built round a courtyard and full of interesting details such as windows half-shuttered in wood (to dodge the window tax), tempera-painted ceilings and a stone-vaulted counting-house. The Town House next door was built in 1626. The Study is an early 17th-century building distinguished by its tower with a little look-out room, and straggling up and down the streets are the so-called 'little houses' of the traders and burghers that give the village its character – white-harled walls beneath grey or red roofs, typical crow-stepped gables, and outside stairs. On the outskirts are the church and ruins of the 13th-century Cistercian abbey.

The Palace, its crow-stepped gables and pantiled roofs characteristic of the local architecture of the period

Wha wad ha' thocht it
Noses wad ha' bocht it?
(Inscription over the old snuffmaker's house, at the top of Tanhouse Brae, dated 1673).

Low tide in a resort whose sands are said to hold garnets

ELIE

Fife

8 MILES (13 KM) EAST OF LEVEN

Elie is another of the string of old ports dotted along the coast of Fife that used to trade extensively with cities across the North Sea. Nowadays its safe, sandy beaches are popular in summer with windsurfers and sailors, and many of the attractive old grey stone fishermen's cottages are holiday homes. The bar of the Ship Inn by the harbour has a collection of old pictures of Elie which show how little its layout and buildings have changed over the years. The old granary building on the harbour is being developed to provide a focal point for watersports, and some accommodation. The ground plan of the village is typical of the East Neuk villages, with one main street and narrow wynds leading down to the sea. William Scott of Ardross built the church in 1639 using the T-plan, common in Scotland at the time, that put the pulpit rather than the altar in the centre of the building. The large house in South Street known as The Castle is also of 17th-century date. To the east, towards the East Links golf course, is the lighthouse and Lady's Tower, built as a summerhouse in 1679 for the wife of a local laird, Lady Jane Anstruther. Elie is virtually one and the same place with Earlsferry, whose people, the legend goes, helped Macduff escape from Macbeth.

Lady Jane Anstruther, known as Jenny Falls, used to hold poetry evenings and soirées in her summerhouse by the sea. At the bottom of the tower was her changing room, from which she would emerge to swim naked in the sea, protecting her modesty by sending a bellringer out to warn villagers to keep away.

KINGHORN

Fife

2 MILES (3 KM) EAST OF BURNTISLAND

A family picnic on the beach at Kinghorn, with the town in the background

Rossend Castle at Burntisland is linked with a tale of Mary, Queen of Scots. French poet Pierre de Châtelard fell extravagantly in love with her and wrote passionate verse in her praise. One night he hid under her bed. Discovered, he was ordered to leave court, but he followed the queen to St Andrews and burst into her bedroom there. He was executed in the market square of St Andrews, crying out just before he died, `Adieu, the most beautiful and the most cruel princess in the world.'

Along the southern shore of the ancient kingdom of Fife stretches a string of little harbours which once supported ports and fishing fleets, but which cater nowadays to holidaymakers and retired people. Kinghorn has a fine spread of sands along Pettycur Bay and good golfing on the links. It was a royal town in the 13th century, and King Alexander III was riding home from Edinburgh here to his beautiful French queen one stormy March night in 1286, when his horse stumbled and he fell to his death over the cliff. A monument was erected 600 years later on the fateful spot, for the king's broken neck was to open the way for Edward I of England to claim authority over Scotland. Further on to the west, Burntisland once had a whaling fleet and a ferry across the Forth to Granton, which ran until 1939. The remarkable church of St Columba with its octagonal tower was the first to be built in Scotland after the Reformation, in 1592. Going the opposite way, east from Kinghorn, Kirkcaldy is the largest town of this region, at the centre of the Fife coalfield and the local lino industry. The excellent town art gallery has a distinguished collection of work by Scottish artists.

FALKLAND PALACE

Fife

FALKLAND, 4½ MILES (7 KM) NORTH-WEST OF GLEN ROTHES

The forbidding walls of Falkland Palace – likened by Thomas Carlyle to 'a black old bit of coffin or protrusive shin-bone sticking through the soil of the dead past' – encapsulate one of the most romantic periods of Scottish history. Here you will find tales of intrigue and murder, of hunting and hawking, of art and of literature.

This was the favourite home of the Stuart kings from the time of James II (of Scotland) until 1651, when Charles II left the palace to face defeat and exile. The fate of the palace at that time was equally dismal; it was occupied by Cromwell's troops, damaged by fire and allowed to fall into ruin.

In 1887, though, the 3rd Marquess of Bute, a descendant of the Royal Stuarts, became Hereditary Keeper of the palace. He restored and rebuilt much of the palace and, though it is now in the care of the National Trust for Scotland, his descendant still lives in the building as Keeper. Inside, it is furnished with huge old oak furniture, including a great four-poster bed said to have belonged to James VI, and rich wall hangings. The old library has a remarkable *trompe-l'oeil* ceiling and there are 17th-century Flemish 'Verdure' tapestries along the gallery leading to the King's apartments.

Open from April to October daily. Tel: 01337 857397.

Falkland Palace has a unique royal tennis court which was built for James V in 1539 and pre-dates Henry VIII's court at Hampton Court Palace by more than 80 years.

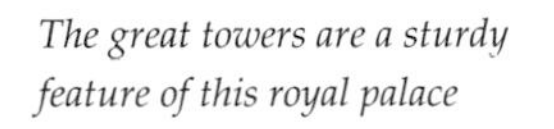

The great towers are a sturdy feature of this royal palace

PITTENWEEM
Fife

10 MILES (16 KM) SOUTH-EAST OF ST ANDREWS

The name is Pictish for 'place of the cave'. In one of the narrow lanes, or wynds, there is, in a rock, the entrance to a series of caves believed to be the home of the 7th-century missionary, St Fillan. Since its re-dedication in the 1930s, the shrine has occasionally been used for underground services. Until the Reformation it was maintained by the monks of the 14th-century Augustinian priory whose ruins may be seen in the grounds of the Episcopal church. The church tower was in fact the tolbooth. Notice its half-glazed, half-shuttered windows. As one of the royal burghs in James VI's 'fringe of gold on a green cloth mantle', Pittenweem held the right to hold markets, and the old mercat cross, symbol of this right, now stands against the tower. Pittenweem has always depended on the sea and today is home to the busy fishing fleet of Fife's East Neuk. It has a covered fish market and its harbour quays are heaped with the usual paraphernalia of fishing. Backing the harbour are some attractive cottages and a group of 16th-century houses called The Gyles. Kellie Lodging in the high street was the 16th-century town house of the earls of Kellie. The Flemish gables seen on several buildings reflect former trading links with the Low Countries.

The gate in the rock that leads to St Fillan's Cave

It was the hanging in Edinburgh of the Pittenweem smuggler, baker Andrew Wilson, that led to the Porteous Riots in 1736, the hot little incident so famously described in Sir Walter Scott's *Heart of Midlothian.* Wilson had become a popular hero by engineering the escape of his accomplice from the Tolbooth. Riots broke out at his hanging and Captain Porteous ordered his troops to fire. Porteous was later lynched by the mob, but so great were the sympathies of high-ranking officials for the rioters that no-one was ever punished.

FORTH RAIL BRIDGE

Fife/Lothian

8 MILES (13 KM) NORTH-WEST OF EDINBURGH

On 4 March 1990 a 53-year-old steam locomotive hauled a special train through the mile-long honeycomb of steel girders and struts across the Forth to mark the centenary of one of the great engineering feats of the Victorian age. The Forth Rail Bridge was designed for the North British Railway by two distinguished engineers, Sir John Fowler and Benjamin Baker, who were also the creators of the Metropolitan Railway in London. It took seven years, 51,000 tons of steel, 7 million rivets and the lives of 57 men to build. The bridge has a surface area of 135 acres (55ha), which a 16-strong team takes 6 years to repaint, starting over again as soon as they have finished. This tremendous construction has stood up to the burden of traffic better than its younger companion, the suspension road bridge which was opened by the Queen in 1964, with towers 512 feet (156m) high and a central span of 3300 feet (1006m). The two bridges replace the ferry which for centuries crossed the river at this point from Queensferry on the southern bank. It was one of the oldest ferry services on record, going back at least 800 to 900 years and involving steamboats, sailing boats and rowing boats in its time.

'To see the Forth Bridge is rather like meeting a popular actress, but with this difference; it exceeds expectations.'
H V Morton, *In Search of Scotland* (1929)

The cantilevered steel bridge disappears into a bank of cloud on its way across the Forth

BO'NESS & KINNEIL RAILWAY

Central

BO'NESS, 15 MILES (24 KM) WEST OF EDINBURGH

The closure of railways in Britain has seldom been accompanied by sensible provisions to safeguard the integrity of the trackbed and structures in case they were needed again. Nontheless, most railway preservation schemes were on the scene quickly enough to prevent the principal buildings being demolished or sold off. A notable exception was the Bo'ness & Kinneil Railway on the southern shore of the Firth of Forth – when the preservationists began work, they lacked even the remains of the trackbed or any foundations on which to rebuild a working railway.

It is a measure of their achievement that Bo'ness station deceives most visitors into thinking that it is the original. The setting is striking: inland the town of stone buildings rises up the hillside, crowned by the villas of the more well-to-do; seaward are the remains of the harbour on which the town's wealth was largely based. At one time 11 miles (17.6km) of sidings covered the waterfront, the wagons filled with coal for export or with

Bo'ness West station; its recreated buildings have won several awards

Acting the part...

imported iron ore and timber. Today the site is home to the largest collection of locomotives, carriages and wagons in Scotland, where most of them were built or worked.

The building that commands admiration is the huge cast- and wrought-iron train shed built in 1842 for Haymarket station in Edinburgh. The rescue of what is one of the finest buildings on any preserved railway was part of the intention to re-create an authentic North British Railway station – that pre-grouping company owned the 4½-mile (7km) line that linked Bo'ness with the Edinburgh–Glasgow main line at Manuel. Before boarding the train, it is worth taking the visitor trail round the goods yard with its wagon turntables, used in restricted sites, and through the vast shed that houses much of the collection.

Pride of place amongst the carriages must go to the Great North of Scotland Railway saloon which was once part of Edward VII's royal train. However, most of the carriages illustrate just how spartan travelling conditions were for third-class passengers until the early years of this century. Locomotives range from main line passenger engines to humble industrial tank engines from the days when large factories and works would be rail connected and have a 'pug', as they were called in Scotland, fussing round the yard.

The booking office at Bo'ness

The start of the 3½-mile (5.5km) journey to Birkhill, the present terminus of the line, passes the dock on the right before the train meanders through a plantation of saplings that now covers the foreshore. Kinneil Halt is used by birdwatchers visiting the adjacent bird sanctuary on the headland. The line forges inland, the deepening bark from the locomotive's exhaust indicating the rising gradient. As the line enters a woodland of ivy-clad trees, it passes close to Kinneil House where an outbuilding was the scene of James Watt's experiments to produce more efficient steam engines.

The ugly sight of Grangemouth oil refinery across the Firth soon disappears from view as the line swings inland and crosses the site of the Antonine Wall, built by the Romans as a bulwark against invasion by the Caledonians. A mile of pastoral landscape precedes arrival at Birkhill, a remote station seemingly offering visitors nothing more than the pretty station building with its oversized cast-iron brackets supporting the canopy. However, to simply return by the next train would be to miss one of the most interesting experiences to be had from a journey on a preserved railway. Behind the station,hidden by trees, are the remains of the boiler house of Birkhill Clay Mine – unremarkable to all except industrial archaeologists, but beyond is an extraordinary sight. The ground drops away to reveal a precipitous gorge through which the River Avon flows.

A long flight of steps parallels a rope-worked inclined plane which hauled small wagons, called hutches, up the hillside from the mine in the valley bottom. At the bottom a bridge over the river leads to the mine entrance. The 6 miles (9.6km) of tunnel were worked as recently as 1980, and retired miners now take parties through some of the workings. Hundreds of feet below the ground torches can pick out the remains of tree trunks that were fossils 170 million years before the first dinosaurs. What was extracted from the mine was turned into firebricks capable of withstanding very high temperatures. They were used in many industries, not least in locomotive boilers. The driver of the locomotive that takes your train back to Bo'ness may let you see the brick arch in the firebox, making an immediate link with the mine and the guide's personal recollections.

Train service: at weekends from April to mid-October; and daily from mid-July to end August. Tel: 01506 822298.

Below: No 239 just arriving at Bo'ness

The ruins of Castle Campbell loom romantically above some of Scotland's finest countryside

CASTLE CAMPBELL

Central

DOLLAR, 10 MILES (16 KM) EAST OF STIRLING

The original name of this stronghold was 'the Castle of Gloume', but the first Earl of Argyll disliked the name and changed it by an Act of Parliament in 1489 to the less dismal Castle Campbell. The castle stands on a rocky spur of land between two streams, rather mournfully named the Burn of Care and the Burn of Sorrow.

It is not known exactly when the first castle was raised here, but the earliest surviving building dates to the end of the 15th century. This fine tower is in an excellent state of preservation, and stands about 60 feet (18m) high to its parapets. It has four storeys, three of which have handsome vaulted ceilings, and there was a pit prison in the basement. During the 16th century the simple tower house was extended to form a quadrangle, although the castle's position on a rocky knoll of land meant that further development was restricted.

During the English Civil War, Castle Campbell's owner, the Earl of Argyll, sided firmly with Cromwell. In 1654 Castle Campbell was burned by Royalists, and in 1661 Argyll was executed. Since then, much of the castle has remained derelict, although the splendid tower house and the east wing were used as a residence by the Argylls until the early 19th century.

Open all year daily in summer, most days in winter. Tel: 0131 668 8800.

Set on a high rock, Stirling Castle has played a major role in Scotland's history

STIRLING CASTLE

Central

STIRLING, 22 MILES (35.5 KM) WEST OF DUNFERMLINE

Perched high and proud on its towering cliffs, Stirling Castle is a complex arrangement of buildings, some plain and functional, others splendid and palatial, that reflect its long history as one of the most important castles in Scotland.

Most of the buildings that can be seen today date from the 15th century or later, and it is not known exactly what the castle was like before this, when it was being fought over by William Wallace, Robert the Bruce and Edward I. This eventful history began in the late 11th century, when a wooden structure was raised. Edward I seized Stirling in 1296 and Wallace took it back in 1297. He lost it again in 1298, but the Scots reclaimed it once more in 1299. Edward retrieved the castle after a furious siege in 1304, and this time held it until the English defeat at Bannockburn in 1314.

There are many fine buildings to explore in this splendid fortress. Perhaps the most impressive is the Great Hall, which is one of the earliest Renaissance buildings in Scotland. The elegant Palace was built for James V in the 1540s, and there are some exquisite carvings, both inside (around the fire-places) and on the exterior walls.

Open all year daily. Tel: 0131 668 8800.

The waters of the River Lochay have since the 1950s been harnessed in one of the Highlands hydro-electric power-stations, named after Finlarig Castle. A pipe-line can be seen from the Glen Lochay road, bringing the water from Glen Lyon that turns the turbines. Finlarig is part of the Tummel Bridge hydro-scheme and is controlled from there.

KILLIN
Central

19 MILES (30.5 KM) NORTH OF CALLANDER

Killin's situation is dramatic. At the western end of Loch Tay – a narrow, deep water that snakes beneath the beckoning slopes of Ben Lawers – it sits just where the Falls of Dochart bring the river crashing and swirling and foaming to meet with the River Lochay, a paradise for walkers, fishermen, yachtsmen and skiers. On the village's south-western outskirts whitewashed cottages line the 18th-century Dochart Bridge near the wooded burial island of the Clan MacNab, the most aggressive of several aggressive clans in the area. Killin's white stone church, rebuilt in 1774, originated in the 9th century and its 10th-century font is the only seven-sided one in Scotland. Just to the north of the village are the overgrown ruins of Finlarig Castle, described in Sir Walter Scott's novel *The Fair Maid of Perth*. This was the stronghold of the Campbells and is associated with the notorious Black Duncan of the Cowl. Close by is his 'beheading pit', perhaps the only surviving example. Upper crust wrong-doers were beheaded in it. Lesser mortals were hanged from a nearby tree. In a field near Breadalbane Park a stone is said to mark the burial place of the 3rd-century Celtic warrior hero, Fingal.

The main street of this summer and winter sports resort, looking towards the green-roofed Episcopal church

Blair, a story-book castle, is set among forested hills above the River Garry

BLAIR CASTLE

Tayside

BLAIR ATHOLL, 8 MILES (13 KM) FROM PITLOCHRY

In 1269 affairs of state forced David, Earl of Atholl, to spend a considerable amount of time in England. While he was away, his neighbour, John Comyn, began to build a castle on Atholl's land, causing Atholl to complain to King Alexander III. This early tower is now incorporated into a much bigger castle, but is still called Cummings (or Comyn's) Tower.

The Earls and Dukes of Atholl were prominent men in Scottish history. The simple tower house was extended and rebuilt over the centuries according to the needs of its different owners. In the English Civil War, Blair, then a fortress with good defences, was captured by Cromwell's forces. In 1745 it was besieged by the Jacobites, in what was probably the last siege to take place in Britain.

Most of the castle as it is seen today dates from the 18th century. It is a splendid palace, its gleaming white walls contrasting starkly with the rich woodland in which it stands. Many richly furnished rooms are open to the public, and some contain objects of great historical significance, including two cannon from an Armada galleon and an original copy of the National Covenant of 1638.

Open from April to October daily. Tel: 01796 481207.

Blair's Private Army

When Queen Victoria came to stay at Blair Castle in 1844, some 200 Athollmen formed a royal bodyguard, so enchanting the young Queen that she presented them with their colours in the following year. As the only private army in the country, the Atholl Highlanders, still recruited largely from the estate, exist today as a ceremonial private bodyguard.

EDZELL CASTLE

Tayside

EDZELL, 8 MILES (13 KM) NORTH OF BRECHIN

The most remarkable feature of this sturdy little fortified tower house is its unusual gardens, complete with bath house and summer house. In 1604 a walled enclosure was added onto the already existing tower house and courtyard, designed to surround one of the most elegant and notable gardens of any castle in western Europe. The garden walls are a triumph in themselves: they have been divided into sections, and are richly adorned with carvings and sculpted panels. Exquisite in their detail, the carvings embrace several themes: the first set depicts a number of planetary deities, including Mars, Jupiter, Venus, and Saturn; the second represents 'the liberal arts'. In medieval learning, the three basic subjects were grammar, rhetoric and logic, while arithmetic, music, geometry and astronomy were the more advanced topics, and each of these is illustrated by seated figures busily practising their art.

The tower house was built in the 15th century as a home for the Lindsay family. Other buildings arranged around a courtyard were added in the 16th century. Edzell saw little military action, although it was occupied by Cromwell's troops in 1651, and was badly damaged in the second Jacobite Uprising in 1747. Today, the tower remains the most complete section, along with the quaint summer house in the south-east corner of the garden.

Open all year daily, except winter Fridays and Christmas. Tel: 0131 668 8800.

Delightful gardens surround this old tower house

Scone Palace is inextricably linked with Scotland's historic past

SCONE PALACE

Tayside

1 MILE (1.5 KM) NORTH OF PERTH

The seat of government in Pictish times, the site of the Stone of Destiny and the place where Scottish kings (including Macbeth and Robert the Bruce) were crowned until 1651 – Scone Palace and the history of Scotland are inextricably linked. Here, great and decisive events took place and powerful men shaped the future. And yet, once the Stone of Destiny had been removed to London, the heart and the power seemed gradually to seep away until, in 1559, the abbey was destroyed by an unruly mob, stirred up by an inflammatory speech by John Knox.

After this, Scone was given to Sir David Murray (later Lord Scone and Viscount Stormont), whose descendants still live there. It was his grandson, the 3rd Earl, who created the Scone Palace we see today, though it was 'Gothicised' in the early 19th century as a tribute to its monastic origins. A series of elegant, beautifully decorated rooms is on show, but even they are overshadowed by the wonderful collections of porcelain, ivories, 16th-century needlework, French furniture and works of art. But though Scone's historical importance and its unrivalled collections might seem overwhelming, it is still very much a family home, with all the charm that entails.

Open from April to October daily. Tel: 01738 552300.

The Stone of Destiny, or Stone of Scone, was taken to Westminster Abbey by Edward I in 1296 and every monarch since that time has been crowned upon it. A local story maintains that Edward was actually fobbed off with an imitation stone, hastily hacked out by the monks at Scone, and that the original lies hidden somewhere in an underground chamber.

The road east from Forfar follows the valley of the Lunan Water. Near to Guthrie is the House of Pitmuies, one of the loveliest estates in this part of Scotland, already rich in such properties. The harled three-storeyed mansion was rebuilt in 1730 by Mr Ogilvy, and 50 years later records show that the walled garden was in existence. The foundations of the modern garden are most probably Victorian, but the beauty and immaculate condition of the layout today is due to the late Mr Farquhar Ogilvie and his wife, Margaret.

Entering the gardens from the car park, you come first to the kitchen garden, which, in traditional fashion, still provides vegetables, fruit and flowers for the house. Beyond, an archway of weeping pears introduces the central walk of the summer borders, flanked by hedges of red cherries and beds planted with soft-coloured summer flowers. Below the house, and linked by stone steps, are three gardens of great beauty and variety. Around a central fountain, with tall bulrushes and waterlilies, ferns, alpines and mallows grow among the paving, while, on one side of the garden are exquisite old-fashioned roses and long beds of massed delphiniums, including some

HOUSE OF PITMUIES

Tayside

GUTHRIE, 8 MILES (13 KM) EAST OF FORFAR

varieties which have been at Pitmuies for more than 70 years. A rambling-rose hedge separates the Rose Garden from the yellow and blue borders which lead back to the house.

Along the Trellis Walk, clematis and climbing roses contrast with blue Himalayan poppies, and ferns, hostas and bergenias flourish close to a row of Tibetan cherry trees. Pinks and violas brighten the paved area and, in raised beds, there is a collection of old and modern cinquefoils. In the Alpine Meadow, which was once the drying ground for the 18th-century 'Gothick' wash-house, autumn mowing encourages a marvellous display of snowdrops and crocuses in spring. By early summer shrub roses and penstemons border the terrace walk which leads to the Turbie Burn. Between the Burn and the Vinny Water, beeches and limes shade the walk, overlooked by an extraordinary turreted dovecote which bears the date 1643 and the Ogilvy and Guthrie arms. The Vinny Garden has some variegated hollies, a monkey puzzle and a paperbark maple, while the walk down to the Black Loch takes you through woodland interplanted with rhododendrons and azaleas.

Open from April to October, daily. Tel: 01241 828245.

Magnificent, densely packed flower borders are flanked by hedges of red cherry

The former carriage house of the House of Dun is now leased to the last handloom linen weaver working in Britain. Once a widespread occupation, linen weaving has now been taken over by machine-looms in factories, but here Ian Dale continues his craft and produces a fine range of traditional designs.

HOUSE OF DUN

Tayside

4 MILES (6.5 KM) WEST OF MONTROSE

It would be difficult to select a highlight from a tour of the House of Dun, such is the quality and variety of its features and contents.

High on the list would be the building itself – a fine example of the work of William Adam dating from the 1730s – and another contender would be the wonderful plasterwork, which consists of a number of allegorical bas-reliefs, friezes and stucco work, most notable in the Saloon. There follows a series of less imposing, but utterly charming rooms, adorned with fine family portraits, china and clocks.

The bedrooms are also particularly interesting, with some beautiful embroidery, splendid tapestries and early examples of bathroom fittings, including a 19th-century boot bath (which actually looks like a boot) and an early, chain-operated shower bath.

Down in the basement, along with the former Servants' Hall are the Gun and Rod Rooms, complete with all the paraphernalia associated with the sports which once filled the larders. Here also is a delightful little model theatre – 'Mr Riach's Performing Theatre of Arts', which dates back to the 1830s. You can also tour the fully equipped and furnished kitchen and the housekeeper's accommodation. Out in the courtyard, the Gamekeeper's Bothy and the Potting Shed provide an insight into some of the work of the estate.

Open at Easter, then from May to September daily; weekends in October. Tel: 01674 810264.

The fine old House of Dun is in the care of the National Trust for Scotland

A magnificent and mysterious castle, Glamis is the family home of the Queen Mother, and is the birthplace of Princess Margaret

GLAMIS CASTLE

Tayside

GLAMIS, 12 MILES (19 KM) NORTH OF DUNDEE

Legends and myths about Glamis Castle are plentiful. King Malcolm II is said to have been murdered here in the 11th century; Lady Janet Douglas, the widow of the Earl of Glamis, was burned at the stake as a witch by James V in 1540; and there is said to be a secret room where one lord of Glamis played cards with the devil. It is difficult to associate such dark tales with the splendid dark red castle, with its ornate turrets and chimneys.

There was probably a castle at Glamis in the early 14th century, but it was not until after 1376 that the L-plan tower house was built by John Lyon on land presented to him by King Robert II. The Lyon family, now Earls of Strathmore and Kinghorne, have owned the castle ever since.

If Glamis today looks more like a French château than a medieval fortress, then that is because it was extensively restored and developed in the 17th and 18th centuries. The original tower house, although strengthened, heightened, and re-roofed, remains the central part of this rambling palace. Tours of the house range from the medieval hall to the 17th-century chapel, and include is the small suite of rooms used by George VI and his queen.

Open Easter weekend, then from May to September daily except Sunday; by appointment in winter. Tel: 01307 840242/3.

Glamis was one of the childhood homes of Queen Elizabeth, The Queen Mother, who was the youngest daughter of the 14th Earl.

LOCH LEVEN CASTLE

Tayside

KINROSS, 10 MILES (16 KM) NORTH OF DUMFERMLINE

The only way to reach the ancient fortress of Loch Leven is by boat, even though the waters of the loch today are lower than they were in the 14th century when the castle was built. This is because the course of the River Leven was altered in the 19th century, and the level of the loch was lowered as a result. The castle itself is a simple square tower of five storeys, surrounded by a towered wall that was a later addition. The third floor of the tower was possibly where Mary, Queen of Scots was imprisoned between June 1567 and May 1568. There are also the remains of what may have been a private chapel, complete with an altar shelf containing a basin, and a small wall cupboard. IN another window is a closet that may have been used as a strong room in which to store valuables.

Queen Mary was unwell for much of the time she was imprisoned at Loch Leven, and she suffered a miscarriage. She escaped from the castle by befriending the boat keeper, but after the Battle of Langside, during which Mary and her supporters were soundly defeated, she fled the country.

Open from April to September, daily. Tel: 0131 668 8800.

Loch Leven Castle is forever associated with the imprisonment of Mary, Queen of Scots

Huntingtower, in Perthshire, was the scene of a famous royal kidnapping

HUNTINGTOWER

Tayside

2 MILES (3 KM) WEST OF PERTH

Huntingtower is one of the most interesting castles in Scotland. It is essentially two towers joined together as one, but intended to be fully independent of each other. The first tower dates from the 15th century and is three storeys tall. In the late 15th or early 16th century, a second rectangular tower was built, a floor higher than the earlier building. In the 17th century, the space between these two towers was walled in and roofed. This remarkable building still displays some original painted ceilings.

One of the most famous events in Scottish history was the 'Raid of Ruthven', which took place at Huntingtower in August 1582. At that time, the castle was called the House of Ruthven and was owned by the powerful Scottish noble, the Earl of Gowrie. The young King James VI was heavily under the influence of two of Gowrie's rivals, the Duke of Lennox and the Earl of Arran. Gowrie and his ally, the Earl of Mar, persuaded the young King to visit the House of Ruthven and then proclaimed him a prisoner. When Arran tried to free the King, he too was imprisoned. Later, Gowrie was executed, and the King ordered that the name of the castle be changed from Ruthven to Huntingtower.

Open all year, daily except winter Fridays and Christmas. Tel: 0131 668 8800.

A story is told that in the 16th century, the daughter of the 1st Earl of Gowrie fell in love with a man whom her family did not consider a suitable match. The young man was given a room in one tower, while the daughter's bedroom was in the other. The daughter had intended to spend the night with her lover, but hearing her mother's footsteps approaching, fled to the roof and leapt from one tower to the other, a span of 9 feet 4 inches (2.8 m). The gap between the two towers is still called the 'Maiden's Leap'.

CLAYPOTTS CASTLE

Tayside

ABOUT 2 MILES (3 KM) EAST OF DUNDEE

Standing on the fringes of a modern housing estate, Claypotts is one of the finest and most complete examples of a Scottish 'Z-plan' tower house – quite literally, a tower that was built in the shape of a Z. Other popular ground plans of 16th-century Scottish domestic architecture include E-plans, L-plans, and even Y-plans.

Claypotts comprises a square tower, with two round towers diagonally opposite each other, so that one tower adjoins the north-east corner, and the other adjoins the south-west corner. This shape was practical, because it allowed defenders to fire their weapons across all the faces of the main building, making it impossible for attackers to approach too closely without exposing themselves to gunfire. In order to ensure that every possible angle was covered by protective fire, a gun loop was even put in the back of the kitchen fireplace. Although this has been blocked up, it can still be clearly seen.

The arrangement of the three linked towers provided 16 rooms on four floors. The ground floor was used for storerooms and the kitchen, while the upper floors would have provided lavish accommodation for the Laird, his family, and their guests.

Open from April to September, daily. Tel: 0131 668 8800.

Claypotts Castle is an excellent example of a Z-plan tower house

Highland hills rise behind the streets of Braemar

BRAEMAR

Grampian

34 MILES (54.5 KM) NORTH OF BLAIRGOWRIE

This is the Highlands at their ravishing best. Heathery hills, a rocky rushing river, the Cairngorm mountains folding away into an ever more blue distance, a dour grey turreted castle, Highland games; the place reeks of history, and there is more than a whiff of royalty too. The village is made up of two former settlements either side of the Clunie, Roman Catholic Auchendryne and Protestant Castleton. In the second half of the 19th century the village was rebuilt with sturdy stone houses, many of which are today the guest-houses that accommodate visitors to the annual Braemar Gathering, which takes place in Memorial Park. The Invercauld Arms Hotel stands on the spot where the 39th Earl of Mar raised the standard to launch the 1715 Rebellion, proclaiming James VIII and III as king, while in one of the cottages in Castleton Terrace, in August 1881, Robert Louis Stevenson wrote the first part of *Treasure Island*. Near the river bridge is Kindrochit Castle. Malcolm Canmore is believed to have built a fortress here, at a meeting of ways across the hills, in the second half of the 11th century but the present castle was built by the Earl of Mar in 1628. Burnt by the Farquharsons 60 years later, it was rebuilt with turrets and crenellations surrounding the original tower-house.

Tradition has it that way back in the 11th century King Malcolm Canmore held martial contests to find the best men to fight with him against the Normans. Certainly Highland gatherings have been held for centuries. The Braemar Games were established in 1832 and Queen Victoria gave them the royal accolade in 1848. The first Saturday in September here is a colourful day of massed pipe bands, dancing, caber-tossing and other athletic events.

DUNNOTTAR CASTLE

Grampian

1 MILE (1.6 KM) SOUTH-EAST OF STONEHAVEN

On the rugged coastline south of Aberdeen a great stack of rock projects into the stormy North Sea, topped by a jumbled collection of buildings spanning several centuries. Joined to the land by a narrow, crumbling neck of rock, great cliffs protect this natural fortress on all sides, while a thick wall and a gatehouse protect the castle entrance.

The first castle on the site was constructed in the 12th century, but virtually nothing remains of this early building. In the 14th century an L-plan tower house was built by William Keith, the Marischal of Scotland. This building dominates the rest of the castle, its 50 foot (15 m) walls still in good repair, although it is roofless.

More buildings were raised in the 16th century, forming a handsome quadrangular courtyard. Although the emphasis was on comfort, rather than on defence, the castle was equipped with gun ports as a safeguard against possible attack. These were used twice in the Civil War when the castle came under siege, first by the Royalists, and then by Cromwell.

In a dark episode in the castle's history, it was used as a prison for 167 Scottish Presbyterians. These people were crammed into a long, narrow chamber known as the Whigs Vault, and conditions were so appalling that many of them died.

Open all year daily, except winter weekends. Tel: 01569 762173.

Dunnottar Castle squats on top of a vast flat-topped rock, 160ft above the sea

Kildrummy, although ruined since 1717, played an important part in Scottish history

KILDRUMMY CASTLE

Grampian

KILDRUMMY, 15 MILES (24 KM) SOUTH OF HUNTLY

Robert the Bruce was married twice. His first wife was a daughter of the powerful Earl of Mar and his second was from the English de Burgh family. Through his first marriage, Robert came into possession of Kildrummy Castle, and it figured prominently in the Scottish wars of independence against Edward I of England.

Like Stirling and Bothwell castles, Kildrummy changed hands several times, most notably after the siege of 1306. Robert's brother, Nigel, had been left in charge of Kildrummy while other supporters of the defeated Bruce hurried north, away from Edward's advancing troops. When Edward laid siege to Kildrummy, Nigel withstood every assault, and his constant counter-attacks made life in the siege camp unbearable. The castle finally fell because of Osbourne, a treacherous blacksmith who was offered gold in return for setting Kildrummy on fire. The garrison surrendered, and Nigel was later executed at Berwick.

Kildrummy Castle today is a seven-sided enclosure with two round towers, two D-shaped towers and a sturdy gatehouse, very much like the one at Harlech. Today, most of this once mighty fortress exists only as foundations in the grass, although some of the towers have survived to first floor level.

Open April to September daily, and winter weekends. Tel: 0131 668 8800.

PETERHEAD

Grampian

27 MILES (44 KM) NORTH OF ABERDEEN

Old Mr Melancholy

It was at Peterhead late in December 1715 that the Old Pretender, otherwise King James III of England and VIII of Scots, landed for the one and only time on Scottish soil. His standard had been raised at Braemar in September and a small army of Highlanders rallied to it, to fight an inconclusive engagement at Sheriffmuir in November. James was of a pessimistic disposition, nicknamed 'Old Mr Melancholy', and he soon decided that the cause was hopeless and returned to his exile in France. The young George Keith, 5th Earl Marischal, and his younger brother James, who had ardently and imprudently joined the rising, had to flee to the Continent, too, later to distinguish themselves in the service of Frederick the Great of Prussia. Years afterwards, the Earl Marischal made his peace with the government and returned to Inverugie.

Fishing boats jostle in Peterhead's spacious harbour.

In 1990 Peterhead was the premier whitefish port in Europe, with £70 million worth of catches landed in the capacious harbour of Peterhead Bay. Overfishing of cod and haddock, however, and the European Community's quotas to protect stocks have made the future uncertain. The town has a second string to its bow as a supply base for the North Sea oil and gas rigs. Built of the local red granite, Peterhead is Scotland's most easterly town. It owed its early development to the Keith family, Earls Marischal, who once owned vast estates in the north-east. Their castle at Inverugie, outside Peterhead, is now a melancholy ruin. The Arbuthnot Museum illuminates the history of the town, which in the 18th century became for a time a smart spa for upper-crust patrons of its warm springs. The harbour proved a more durable asset, however; in the 1880s a prison was built on the bay and the felons were put to work on harbour improvements. In the 19th century Peterhead became a leading whaling port, later turning to herring fishing, but overfishing put paid to the herring harvest and Peterhead fishermen turned instead to whitefish.

PORTSOY

Grampian

6 MILES (10 KM) WEST OF BANFF

Restored warehouses at Portsoy, once a busy herring port

The coast of the former shire of Banff, with its high cliffs and fishing villages looking out over the Moray Firth to the cold northern seas, has been hopefully christened `the Banffshire Riviera'. This particular stretch of it was dominated by the Ogilvie family. One of them, Patrick Ogilvie, Lord Boyne, built the harbour at Portsoy at the end of the 17th century for the export of Portsoy marble, the red and green serpentine stone found in the cliffs here. As he contrived to persuade the Scots parliament to put a ban on the import of marble from abroad, business was gratifyingly brisk. The ban only lasted for six years, but a profitable export trade to France developed and there is Portsoy marble in chimneypieces at Versailles. The fifth Earl of Seafield built a second harbour in 1828, which was destroyed by the sea and rebuilt, as the village flourished on abundant catches of herring. Today Portsoy is a small resort of character for sailing enthusiasts and holidaymakers. The old warehouses and harbour buildings have been nicely restored and souvenir items are still made of Portsoy marble. Not far to the east are the ruins of the once formidable Ogilvie stronghold of Boyne Castle.

Although William Forbes was not a figure of national significance, he was well respected locally. Generous to local people, by all accounts he was unusually cultured and enlightened for a laird of his time.

TOLQUHON CASTLE

Grampian

PITMEDDEN, 15 MILES (24 KM) NORTH OF ABERDEEN

'All this warke excep the auld tour was begun be William Forbes 15 Aprile 1584 and endit be him 20 October 1589.'

These words are inscribed in a panel high up on the right hand side of the imposing gatehouse at Tolquhon Castle (pronounced 'Tuh-hon'). They refer to the work of the 7th Lord of Tolquhon, the cultured William Forbes, who inherited the castle in the late 16th century. Before Tolquhon came into Forbes' possession, it was little more than a single tower (the 'auld tour') with some adjoining walls. But in 1584, Forbes decided the tower was insufficient for his needs, and set about extending it. The result was the fine palatial building that can be visited today, and although Tolquhon is now a ruin, it takes little imagination to envisage how splendid this castle must have looked in its heyday.

The 'auld tour', or Preston's Tower,

Right, now a roofless ruin, Tolquhon remains an impressive and handsome castle

was raised in the early 15th century, probably by John Preston, its namesake. It was built of granite, with thick walls, and had small rooms which would have been ill-lit and probably cramped for the people living in them. Little remains of Preston's Tower except the vaulted basement and parts of the first floor. Forbes used it as one of the corners of his new castle, and extended the building to make a four-sided structure around a large courtyard. The castle was entered through a gatehouse which, although it appears to be formidable with its gun loops and round towers, had thin walls and would not have withstood a serious attack. It was designed for show, rather than defence.

An impressive array of buildings line all four sides of the fine cobbled courtyard. To the east are the kitchens and an unpleasant pit-prison, while the main house is to the south. This building contained the hall – a spacious, airy room lit by large windows, and the laird's personal chambers, along with additional bed chambers and a gallery. Contemporary records show that William Forbes owned many books, and it is likely that they would have been displayed here.

Forbes' work here did not stop with his fine new house, but extended to the grounds. The hall and his private chamber looked out over a formal garden, and though this has long since disappeared, the remains of a dovecote and recesses for bees have been discovered in the walls.

Open from April to September, daily; weekends only in winter. Tel: 0131 668 8800.

CRATHES CASTLE

Grampian

3 MILES (5 KM) EAST OF BANCHORY

Broad borders almost smother the paths

The first view of Crathes Castle proves that it is all that a Scottish castle should be. The magnificent woodland of Royal Deeside opens up to reveal the romantic tower-house with its turret stairs set in flowing lawns and with eight 'garden rooms', full of colour, contrasting with dark green topiary. It was not until Sir James Burnett and his wife, Sybil, came to Crathes in 1926 that the garden took on its present appearance, and the brilliance of its design and planting is their achievement. Today, the castle and

gardens are under the care of the National Trust for Scotland.

Entering the gardens brings you directly into the White Borders. Beyond the West Border, with its herbaceous plants of blue and pink, steps lead to the Aviary Border, which shows olearias, clematis, *Carpentaria californica* and a splendid *Magnolia wilsonii*. To the right is the Golden Garden, with *Viburnum opulus* 'Xanthocarpum', golden berberis, philadelphus, weigela and the rose 'Agnes', and half-way down the White Borders there is a Portugal laurel, *Prunus lusitanica*, from which point the main herbaceous borders run up to the glasshouses. Here, there are syringas, viburnums and an interesting *Dipteronia sinensis*, while the June borders, with the dovecote as a focal point, are planted in the cottage-garden style, with lupins, bearded irises, pyrethrum and several varieties of Oriental poppies.

The Wild Garden is at its best during the autumn with photinias, osmanthus and *Philadelphus wilsonii* contrasting with sorbus and *Liriodendron tulipifera*. In the Upper Pool Garden, Lady Burnett took the colours yellow, red and bronze, and by combining unlikely plants – for instance old roses with heathers or the yellow *Coreopsis vecticillata* with the bronze-leaved form of the wild bugle – she achieved some remarkable effects. The Rose Garden is formally arranged with four triangular beds holding floribunda roses supported by viburnums, a group of crab apples and a pocket handkerchief tree. Clearly inspired both by Gertrude Jekyll and by Lawrence Johnston at Hidcote, the gardens at Crathes Castle hold many treasures for the plant lover and the garden visitor alike.

Open daily. Tel: 01330 844 651.

A path leads from the Rose Garden towards the extravagant topiary

SHIELDAIG

Highland

9 MILES (15 KM) NORTH OF KISHORN

The harbour at Shieldaig, suspended between blue sky and blue water

Vying with Plockton as one of the most attractive villages in the Highlands, Shieldaig, with its white-harled and slate-roofed cottages, lies close to the head of Loch Shieldaig in some of Scotland's most breath-taking scenery. The buildingof roads since World War II has made this area much more accessible to visitors, for good or ill. Loch Shieldaig was always known for its herrings, though no longer, and indeed the name was originally Sildvik, which is Norse for `herring bay'. The loch opens into Loch Torridon, by common consent one of the most magical of all Scotland's beautiful sea lochs. To the south lie the mountains, moors and deer forest of the Applecross Peninsula, and a coast road, opened in 1976 to link the scattered crofting settlements together, commanding views over the Inner Sound to Raasay and Skye. Going the other way, east from Shieldaig, the A896 road along Upper Loch Torridon yields awesome prospects of the red sandstone crags of Beinn Alligin and Liathach, rising above 3000 feet (915m). The National Trust for Scotland owns the superb 16,000-acre (6,500ha) Torridon Forest estate, which formerly belonged to the Earls of Lovelace, with its rare eagles and wildcats, deer and mountain goats. There is a good visitor centre and a deer museum.

GAIRLOCH
Highland

7 MILES (11 KM) NORTH-WEST OF KINLOCHEWE

As late as 1960 Gairloch still made its living from the sea, as the Minch fishing boats landed their catches at the pier. Today it is a holiday resort and a centre for touring the wild and dramatic mountains of Wester Ross. Beside the loch of the same name, the village has a sandy beach and there are sailing and sea angling trips to be enjoyed, while the Heritage Museum has a rich store of information about such matters as illicit whisky stills. Loch Gairloch is geologically interesting because it displays the two principal rock types of the north-western coastline. The northern shore is made of reddish Torridonian sandstone, but the southern shoreline is grey Lewisian gneiss. There are sandy beaches along the northern shore, and a coast road leads up to Melvaig with sea views to Skye and the Outer Hebrides. The A832 leads north-east from Gairloch to Poolewe, for boat trips on Loch Ewe and the fabulous Inverewe Gardens (National Trust for Scotland) on the bank of the loch. To the south-east is the beautiful 12-mile stretch of Loch Maree, with the great peak of the Slioch rising above 3,000ft (915m) on its northern side.

Gairloch lies scattered over its greensward, with the loch and mountains beyond

STRATHSPEY RAILWAY

Highland

AVIEMORE, 29 MILES (46.5 KM) SOUTH OF INVERNESS

This line follows the valley of the River Spey, with the Cairngorm Mountains rising to the south-east. Since the growth of winter sports in Scotland during the late 1960s, Aviemore has become the major centre for skiing, a network of chairlifts serving slopes around the small town. Until then it was known for little more than being an important junction on the railway between Perth and Inverness, where trains went either directly to Inverness over Slochd summit or took the circuitous route through Forres and Nairn. Passenger services over the latter were withdrawn in 1965, but preservationists and the Highlands & Islands Development Board wanted to save the 5-mile (8km) section between Aviemore and the tranquil village of Boat of Garten.

Their efforts came to fruition in 1978 when regular services were resumed during the tourist season. Unfortunately Strathspey Railway trains are unable to run into the British Rail station, but it is only a short walk between the two. The Strathspey has created an authentic feel to its Aviemore station by re-erecting railway buildings of the former Highland and Great North of Scotland railways, which served the area before the 1922 grouping. It has one of the finest locomotive sheds on any preserved railway – a solid stone four-track shed, which became a garage after its closure in around 1966

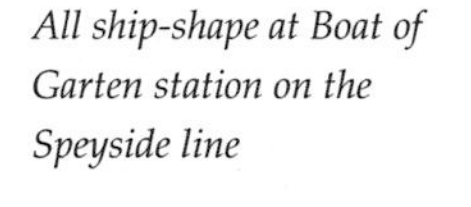

All ship-shape at Boat of Garten station on the Speyside line

No doubt as to the owners of this handsome locomotive here at Aviemore

but was returned to its rightful use by the Strathspey Railway, and it can be seen to the east as the train pulls out of Aviemore for the 20-minute journey.

Once over a level crossing serving the holiday village at Dalfaber, the line is into open country with fine views of the Cairngorm mountains to the east and the Monadhliaths to the west. Clumps of trees sometimes indicate surviving remnants of the Caledonian Forest that once covered the area. Silver birches accompany the approach to Boat of Garten, where it is worth spending some time.

The former junction for the Speyside line to Craigellachie today offers a railway museum, and the Strathspey Railway's excellent guide book suggests two walks from the station. You can also take a vintage coach to an observation hide provided by the Royal Society for the Protection of Birds that overlooks Loch Garten; since the 1950s this has been home to ospreys that have returned here each year from their winter refuge in Africa.

Train service: daily in July and August, and most days in June and September, also on selected days in April, May and October. Santa specials. Tel: 01479 810725.

SOUTH-EAST SUTHERLAND

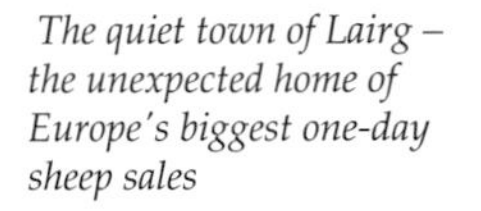

This part of Sutherland is an area of contrasts, clearly shown on this 69-mile (111km) planned tour. Sandy beaches separate holiday resorts on the coast. Inland there are huge areas of sheep farms and deer forests. Two vastly wealthy men – a duke and an industrialist – cast very different shadows.

DIRECTIONS

Leave Dornoch on the A949 Castle Street, and at the war memorial turn right on to the B9168 (sp. Wick). After a further 2 miles turn right on to the A9. Continue on the A9 and cross the head of Loch Fleet by a causeway, The Mound. Continue into Golspie. Continue on the A9 past Dunrobin Castle and Cairn Liath and on along the coast of Brora. Pass the clock tower, then cross the river bridge and turn left, unclassified (no signs). Continue as the road becomes a single track. Pass through Rogart and, at the main road, turn right on to the A839 (sp. Lairg). In Lairg follow the Lochinver signs and turn right across the River Shin to leave by the A839. In ¾ mile branch left on to the B864 (sp. Inveran) and follow a single-track road through Achany Glen and past the Falls of Shin. Continue on the B864, and in 1¼ miles turn left on to the A837 (sp. Bonar Bridge) and re-cross the River Shin. After ½ mile join the A836 for Invershin and continue to Bonar Bridge. Here turn left on to the A9 (sp. Wick), passing by Spinningdale to reach Clashmore. In ¼ mile turn left at the junction of the A9 and the new approach road from the Dornoch Firth Bridge Road. Continue for 1¼ miles and turn right onto the A949 for the return to Dornoch.

The quiet town of Lairg – the unexpected home of Europe's biggest one-day sheep sales

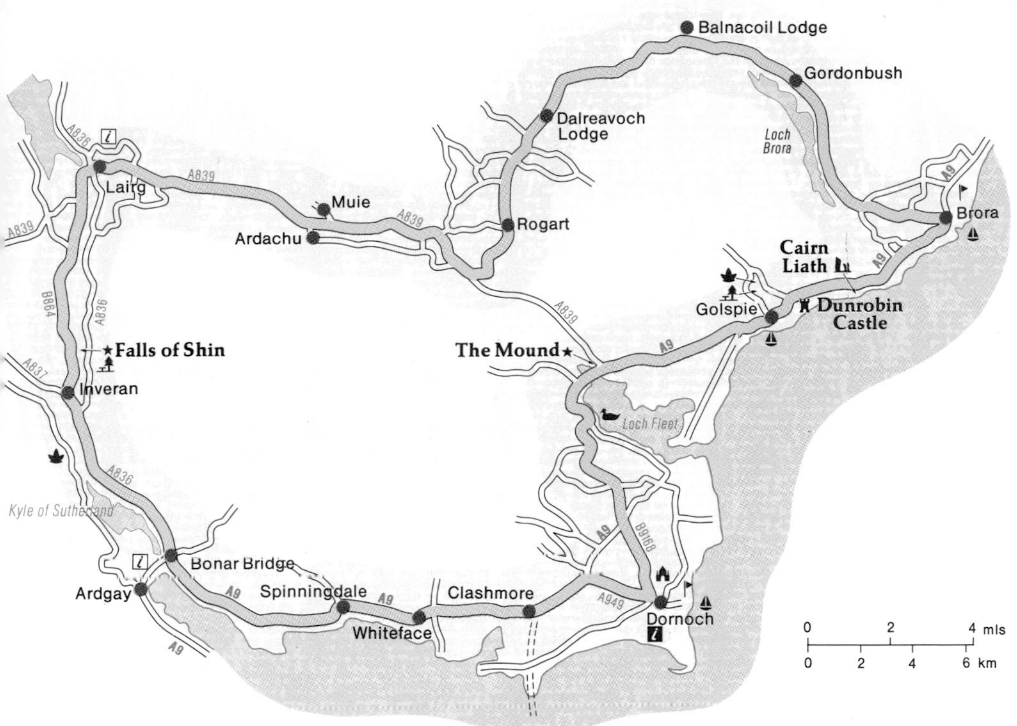

ON THE TOUR

Dornoch

Golfers come to Dornoch from all over the world. The Royal Dornoch course lies between a long sandy beach and colourful banks of gorse. A footpath overlooks it on the way to Embo. In the attractive square, Dornoch Cathedral was first used for worship in 1239. One group of stained glass windows commemorates Andrew Carnegie, the multi-millionaire philanthropist who retired from business in America to spend most of his time at nearby Skibo Castle. In a garden in the Littletown district, a stone marks the spot where in 1722 poor, demented Janet Horne was the last 'witch' burned in Scotland.

The craft centre in the square at Dornoch is also the entrance to the old town jail. There are displays in most of the original cells. An unusual workshop in the industrial estate at the Dornoch station site makes boomerangs.

The Mound

In 1816 Thomas Telford's causeways and bridge over the river Fleet here made the dangerous ferries on the coastal route redundant. Later, The Mound was also used by the Dornoch Light Railway, which branched off the main line to the north.

Golspie

Created from a few fishing huts to house victims of the Sutherland clearances, Golspie is now a comfortable town with a long beach and a golf course, as well as magnificent walks around the waterfalls in Dunrobin Glen. St Andrew's church dates from the 16th century and includes the 'laird's loft' of the Sutherland family.

Dunrobin Castle

In mid-Victorian times the second Duke of Sutherland commissioned Sir Charles Barry, architect of the House of Commons, to remodel the ancient family seat. It was originally a square keep, but as it now stands, Dunrobin is almost a palace in the French style, and the grandest house in the north of Scotland. It has many public rooms, a museum and smaller displays including the estate's old steam-powered fire engine. Beautiful formal gardens border the sea.

Brora

A mixture of holiday resort and industrial town, Brora has an exhilarating, breezy beach, a good golf course and excellent salmon fishing, as well as a malt whisky distillery and a woollen mill to visit.There are many interesting Pictish sites to visit in the surrounding area.

Rogart

A scattered crofting village in a maze of roads above the upper valley of the River Fleet, Rogart is a stop on the long Lairg loop of the Inverness-to-Thurso railway. There is a monument to Sir John Macdonald, first prime minister of Canada. His family originated in the area and were among those turned out at the time of the Clearances.

Lairg

This road-junction village and popular angling centre holds the biggest one-day sheep sales in Europe. The countryside is wild and beautiful, including forests. The dammed waters of Loch Shin power a hydroelectric station. The little hill known as The Ord is a good viewpoint, and the site of many ancient habitations.

Bonar Bridge

Telford built the first bridge over the Kyle of Sutherland here, but the modern structure dates from 1973. Salmon in great numbers swim through the narrows on their way to the spawning grounds, and the Kyle is also a fine sea trout water. Fish passes here allow the salmon free passage upstream; there is a famous salmon leap at the Falls of Shin.

CAWDOR CASTLE

Highland

CAWDOR, 6 MILES (10 KM) SOUTH-WEST OF NAIRN

Cawdor Castle has had a violent history. It was home to the Thanes of Cawdor, who played an active role in local Scottish politics throughout the centuries, but the 9th Thane was branded on the hip with a hot key as a child, and both the 4th and the 11th Thanes were murdered.

Cawdor is also associated with Macbeth's murder of King Duncan, but as Macbeth lived during the 11th century, and Cawdor was not built until the 14th century, the link between Duncan's bloody murder and Cawdor Castle may be poetic licence.

Nevertheless, the appearance of the austere tower and battlements make it easy to imagine why Shakespeare chose it as the location for his grim tale of madness and regicide. The keep dates from the 15th century, and is a forbidding grey tower with walls 11 feet (3.4 m) thick in places, once surrounded by a deep ditch. The later buildings sprout an attractive array of steep-sided roofs, crow-stepped gables, and small turrets dating from the 17th and 19th centuries. Inside, visitors can explore parts of the keep and rooms in the later buildings. There is a fine 17th-century kitchen displaying an array of antique household utensils, and bedrooms containing an elegant Georgian bed and an exquisite Flemish tapestry.

Open daily from May to October. Tel: 01667 404615.

The castle is the ancient seat of the Thanes of Cawdor

Almost more like some Alpine château, Dunrobin stands high on an outcrop

DUNROBIN CASTLE

Highland

1 MILE (1.5 KM) NORTH-EAST OF GOLSPIE

Dunrobin is named after Earl Robin who built the original castle – a great square keep looking out over the sea from its cliff-top vantage point – here in the 13th century. The present Dunrobin Castle bears little resemblance, though, to that original tower, since it was rebuilt in the 19th century in the romantic Gothic style to a design by Sir Charles Barry (who also designed the Houses of Parliament).

With its gleaming towers and turrets, the seat of the Dukes of Sutherland certainly strikes a magnificent pose and is all the more interesting because older parts of the castle can still be distinguished amidst the Victorian building.

The interiors are no less impressive, with beautiful rooms furnished with fine French furniture, tapestries and paintings, including works by Canaletto. Many of the rooms, including the drawing room, dining room and library, reflect the involvement here of architect Sir Robert Lorimer in the early part of this century. He was a leading light in the Arts and Crafts movement, as the standard of workmanship ably demonstrates.

The castle is set in beautiful gardens which were laid out in grand style in the 19th century. The influence of Versailles on the garden design is unmistakable.

Open Easter, then mid-May to mid-October daily. Tel: 01408 633177.

ARDVRECK CASTLE

Highland

26 MILES (41.5 KM) NORTH-EAST OF ULLAPOOL

When Civil War broke out in England in 1642, Scotland was inevitably drawn into the conflict. Two of the main protagonists in the north were Archibald Campbell, Marquess of Argyll, and James Graham, Marquess of Montrose. Montrose remained loyal to the King, while Argyll declared for Parliament. After the execution of Charles I in 1649, Montrose fled the country, but returned a year later. He was captured by the Laird of Assynt, who held him in Ardvreck Castle until he could be safely handed over to Cromwell's forces. Montrose was hastily executed in the same year, while his rival, Argyll, was executed after the Restoration of the monarchy in 1661.

The small 16th-century tower house is now a ruin, perched on a rocky peninsula that juts out into Loch Assynt. It was a simple structure – rectangular, with a staircase turret on the south-east corner. The basement had three chambers with vaulted roofs. One of the chambers is little more than a passage, but the gun loops pierced in its outer wall suggests that it could have been used to defend the castle. When observing Ardvreck Castle, visitors may notice some other ruins nearby. These are the remains of Edderchalder House, a fine 17th-century mansion.

The castle can be seen from the A837, and is best admired from a distance – the ruins are in a dangerous condition.

Ardvreck Castle stands in a wonderful setting by the waters of Loch Assynt

The beautiful Eilean Donan Castle stands guard on a promontory where three lochs meet

EILEAN DONAN CASTLE

Highland

DORNIE, 8 MILES (13 KM) EAST OF KYLE OF LOCHALSH

Dwarfed by the brooding hills surrounding Loch Duich, the castle of Eilean Donan stands picturesquely on its rocky island. A fortress was built here in 1220 by Alexander II to protect himself against raids by Vikings. During the Jacobite Rebellion the Macraes, owners of the castle, opted to support the Old Pretender and garrisoned a small force of Spanish soldiers here. In 1719 the guns of an English man-of-war pounded the castle to pieces.

It remained in ruins until 1912, when Colonel John Macrae decided to restore his ancestral home. Paying great attention to detail, the lakeside castle was lovingly rebuilt, along with an arched bridge that affords easier access to the castle than the ancient Macraes would have known.

Some rooms in the castle are open to visitors, all furnished in the style of the home of a country laird. There are fine collections of pistols and powder horns, and, although it is mostly a 20th-century restoration, it allows the imagination to return to the time when it was owned by the wild Macraes. A fearsome clan, they relished the displaying of the heads of their enemies from the battlements, and local legends tell how, on one occasion, they defended the castle successfully when outnumbered by their attackers 400-to-one.

Open from April to September daily. Tel: 01599 555202.

HOLBORN HEAD

Caithness Sandstone

The sandstone of Holborn Head has been quarried since the early 19th century to provide the famous Caithness flagstones; these have been exported to many parts of Britain, including London, to make paving stones. Locally they are used to make the characteristic flagstone fences; in a treeless landscape they make a cheap and efficient material for field boundaries. Where the sandstone is exposed on cliffs and isolated stacks, its horizontal bedding provides superb nesting ledges for seabirds.

Some of Britain's stormiest waters lie between Caithness and Orkney. The meeting of several tides and currents in these narrow straits north of Holborn Head leads to severe turbulence; add the strong winds which seem to blow permanently, and all the ingredients for rough seas are present. The power of the sea has eroded the rock to form some dramatic cliff scenery: many stacks, gulleys, arches and caves are arranged around the headland. Holborn Head lies about 2 miles (3.2km) north-west of Thurso. The walk is approximately 4½ miles (7.2km) long, and starts from Scrabster Harbour car park. It is mostly easy walking, but some sections are on the edge of sheer cliffs, so take care not to stray off the path, especially in windy weather. There are spectacular views of the wild Caithness coastline and the Orkney Islands.

DIRECTIONS

1 From Scrabster Harbour take the harbour road towards the lighthouse. In winter check the inner harbour for gulls, including glaucous gulls, and divers. Further along the road towards the lighthouse, scan the rocks below for waders like turnstones, and watch for divers and black guillemots in the bay.

2 Just before the lighthouse, take a path to the left, passing through a gate and following the path up the hill. The grassy path then leads along the cliff-top to Holborn Head, crossing two stiles on the way.

Look out for skylarks and pipits in the fields and, in winter, flocks of lapwings and golden plovers. In summer, seabirds will be seen on the cliffs below. Kittiwakes are small, dainty gulls with black-tipped wings and a 'kitt-e wake' call. They nest in small, noisy colonies along the cliffs.

3 At the headland are the remains of an Iron Age fort, built in a strategic position over-looking sheer cliffs on one side and an easily defended narrow neck of land on the other. A wall was built across the neck of land as a further defence. From the headland it is possible to look across the Pentland Firth and see large numbers of seabirds in summer; watch fishing boats in case unusual gull species are following them. Pilot whales, white-sided dolphins and common porpoises are seen out to sea and the appearance of a large number of seabirds, especially gannets, feeding excitedly on a shoal of fish is usually a good pointer to where these small whales may appear at the surface.

Bringing the catch ashore at Scrabster

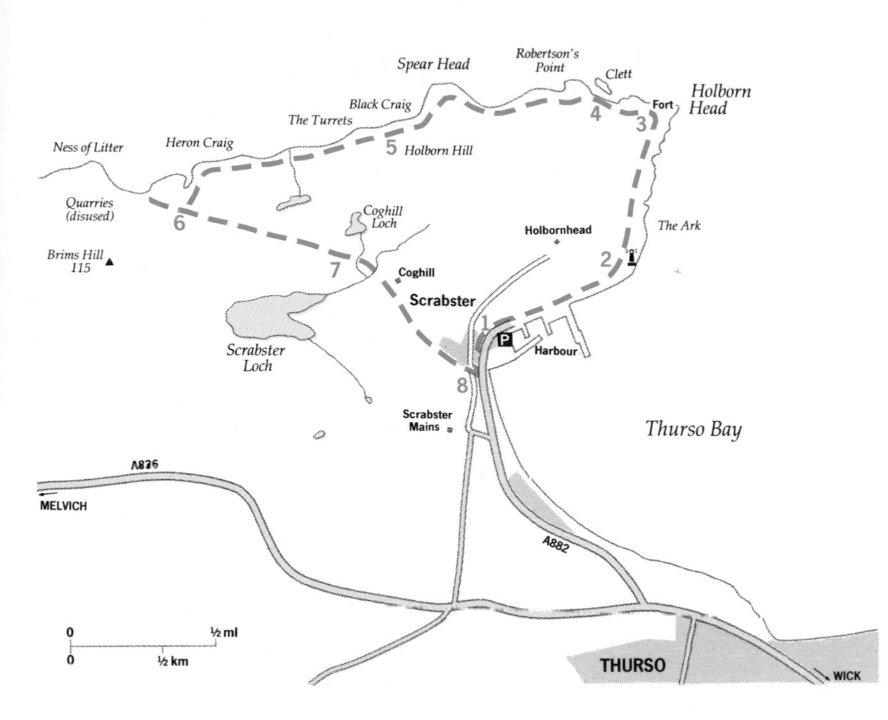

Winter Migrants

In winter a new population of birds appears and, although the nesting ledges may be deserted, the harbour and Thurso Bay will have many divers, sea ducks and gulls over-wintering. Many of these will be from the far north; Iceland gulls, which actually breed in Greenland, large pale-winged glaucous gulls, and the tiny and very rare Ross's gull all turn up from time to time. The sandy beaches and exposed rocks are home to large numbers of waders, especially dunlins, turnstones, sanderlings and redshanks, and rock pipits and snow buntings feed along the high-tide line.

4 Return to the main cliff-top path from the headland, keeping the caves on the right and the wire fence on the left. Beyond the caves, cross the fence for safety as the cliffs here are steep. Continue heading west, with the wire fence on your right.

In summer check the short turf for wild flowers, but be very careful near the edge. The huge rock stack set off from the main cliff is the Clett – a superb nesting habitat for seabirds like fulmars, guillemots and puffins. They are present in summer during the breeding season, but there is so much competition for good nesting ledges that some birds, especially fulmars, visit in the winter to claim to a prime nesting site.

5 Cross the stile in the stone wall and keep straight on towards the quarries; keep to the inland side of the wire fence for safety. Where it is safe to do so, scan the cliffs through binoculars to look for nesting seabirds. Check the rough ground inland on Holborn Hill for short-eared owls and flocks of waders in winter. Look out for the flagstone fences; the pure, damp air of Caithness is ideal for lichens, and many species have colonised these exposed stones.

6 On reaching the gravel road, turn right towards the old quarry; go through the gate and then turn right. This is a good place to look at the Caithness flagstone and see how it was quarried. From the edge of the quarry there is a good view of some sections of the cliff with nesting seabirds. Check the sheltered spots below the cliffs for sea ducks in winter. Take care near the cliff-edge.

7 Return to the gravel road and follow it for about a mile towards Scrabster. On the right is Scrabster Loch and a number of smaller shadow pools, which may hold birds in winter and summer; try not to disturb nesting birds in the breeding season.

8 The gravel road joins a tarmac road which should be followed as far as a postbox. Turn sharp left here, then right down some steps to reach the main road which leads back to the car park at Scrabster Harbour.

❀

BIRDLIFE

Although these rough waters are a hazard to sailors, they are not as damaging to wildlife as might be expected. Ocean currents bring a constant supply of food, and these cold northern waters are a fertile feeding ground for fish, birds and sea mammals. The steep cliffs, with their multitude of nesting ledges, provide ideal conditions for seabirds, and large colonies are found along this coast.

The larger gulls and kittiwakes are present everywhere, following the fishing boats in and out of harbour and loafing in large flocks on half-tide rocks. Guillemots, razorbills and puffins crowd the rock ledges, crevices and grassy cliff-tops in early summer and fly out to the deeper waters of the Firth to feed on sand eels. Fulmars make use of the updraughts on the cliffs to glide and wheel past their nesting ledges, and the occasional great or arctic skua visits from nesting colonies on Hoy. The largest British seabird of all, the gannet, with a 6ft (1.8m) wingspan, is often seen off shore, although none nests on the mainland cliffs.

Above and right, Urquhart is a famous landmark on the shores of Loch Ness

URQUHART CASTLE
Highland

DRUMNADROCHIT, 16 MILES (26 KM) SOUTH-WEST OF INVERNESS

In 1545 the fearsome Macdonald clan swept into the quiet Glen of Urquhart, looting and pillaging as they went. They laid siege to the castle and plundered it mercilessly, taking chairs, tables, gates, armour, food and even the pillows from the beds. After the castle had been thoroughly sacked, the raiders turned their attention to the homesteads in the valley. This was just one incident in a long history of warfare and bloodshed that had raged since a castle was first built on the shores of Loch Ness in the early 13th century. The first recorded owner of the castle was Alan Durward, Lord of Atholl. Durward's brother-in-law was Alexander II, King of Scotland, and it would seem that the young king was very much under the influence of his powerful relative.

In 1296 Edward I of England seized Urquhart along with other castles in the area, but his hold was precarious and he lost it again by 1303. Edward marched north and retook the castle,

but within five years Robert the Bruce had attacked Edward's garrison and secured Urquhart for himself.

Although Urquhart remained in the hands of the Scottish government during the 14th and 15th centuries, it was not an easy ownership. Not only was the castle under threat from the English, but there was a constant threat of attack from the Lords of the Isles. These fiercely independent people had been forced into the Kingdom of Scotland after the Battle of Largs in 1263, and were so keen to regain their freedom that they even sided with the English. Urquhart passed from the Lords of the Isles to the Scottish government and back again in a long series of bloody encounters that continued until the Lordship of the Isles no longer existed.

In view of its turbulent history, it is not surprising that Urquhart's defences are formidable. A walled causeway, with a drawbridge halfway along, led to the castle gatehouse. Great walls that followed the contours of the rock protected it from attack, strengthened by a ditch at the front and the loch at the back. Inside the walls were a variety of buildings, including living quarters, a chapel, kitchens and a dovecote. Although much is ruined, apart from the 16th-century tower house which is still largely intact, this romantic ruin huddled on the loch shore is well worth a visit.

Open all year daily, except Christ mas and January. Tel: 0131 668 8800.

Looking for the Monster

Visitors to Loch Ness may be more familiar with the tales of the monster than with Urquhart Castle. 'Nessie' first made an appearance to a monk in the 8th century, and many hundreds of people have claimed to have seen it since, especially during the last 100 years or so. Eye-witness accounts do not readily agree – it has variously been described as a coiled serpent and as a great crocodile.

'The lonely sea and the sky' – the Sutherland shore at Scourie

SCOURIE

Highland

5 MILES (8 KM) WEST OF LAXFORD BRIDGE

On this desolate stretch of the Sutherland coast the village is a welcome base for bird-watchers, walkers and anglers in quest of the trout in the region's numerous lochs. Lying offshore is Handa Island, reached by boat from Scourie or Tarbet, an important nature reserve which is now managed by the Scottish Wildlife Trust. Seabirds nest in their tens of thousands on the towering sandstone cliffs – herring gulls and black-headed gulls, guillemots, razorbills, kittiwakes and shags. There are Arctic and great skuas, too, and barnacle geese are seen here in winter. Bird's eggs, fish and potatoes used to be the diet of the island's hardy seven-family population, who had their own 'queen' – the oldest widow. The potato famine of the 1840s drove them away and Handa has ever since been left to the wheeling gulls. This part of the coast running up to Cape Wrath is made mainly of Lewisian gneiss of astounding antiquity. Rocks at Scourie have been dated at nearly 3,000 million years old. It is a country of deep sea lochs and inlets, sandy bays, scattered small islands and very few roads. Grey seals are a familiar sight offshore and in Loch Lexford, with boat trips from Fanagmore to see them. Further north, Kinlochbervie on Loch Inchard developed as a fishing port after World War II.

JOHN o' GROATS

Highland

2 MILES (3 KM) WEST OF DUNCANSBY HEAD

Everyone knows that John o' Groats is the most northerly point of the British mainland, corresponding to Land's End at the south-western tip, some 870 miles (1,400km) away. Strictly speaking, everyone is wrong, as the real northernmost point is Dunnet Head, whose great cliffs rise imposingly above the Pentland Firth some 2 miles (3km) closer to the North Pole. However, the hotel at John o' Groats – there is not much else there – is where the tourists go and where the races and charity walks start or finish. In 1990, when Peter de Savary became the first person ever to own both Land's End and John o' Groats, there were plans for tourist development of the latter, but these did not materialise. John o' Groats commands a view over to the cliffs of Orkney on a clear day. The place takes its name from a Dutchman named Jan de Groot, who operated a ferry from here to South Ronaldsay in the 1490s; or, in another explanation of the name, it is said that the fare was a groat. A mound by the hotel is supposed to be the site of his house. There are boat trips in summer to view the beetling cliffs and the seabirds at Duncansby Head, at Scotland's north-eastern corner, and to the deserted island of Stroma.

The Turning Point

The Pentland Firth, earlier known as the Pictland Firth, is about 14 miles long and from 6 to 8 miles broad. It is a tumultuous and dangerous piece of water, known for sunken reefs and whirlpools, where opposing currents smack into each other to send gouts of water high into the air. Windows in the lighthouse on Dunnet Head, more than 300 feet (90m) above the sea, have been smashed by stones flung up by the raging waves below. At the western end of the firth, however, Cape Wrath was not named for the fury of the sea. Wrath is a corruption of the Norse word *hvarf*, meaning 'turning point', for this was where the Viking longships turned south to range down Scotland's west coast.

Flying the flag for Scotland: the 1870s John o' Groats Hotel

NATIONAL PARKS

ALL OR NOTHING ?

Few people would dispute the fact that the finest wilderness areas in Britain are north of the Border, in Scotland. Yet on the surface it seems a strange paradox that, some 40 years after National Parks were first designated in England and Wales, there are still none in Scotland. To look for the reasons for this apparent anomaly we need to go back into the complicated history of countryside conservation and access in Britain, which developed quite differently on both sides of the Border.

By strange irony, John Muir – one of the greatest pioneers of the original American National Park movement – was a Scot, born in Dunbar, and the first Parliamentary attempt to gain walkers legally-protected access to mountain and moorland in Britain a century ago was prompted by the deteriorating access situation in Scotland. This followed the barbarous Highland Clearances, the introduction of vast sheep farms, and the increasing financial importance to landowners of deer stalking. When the Scottish Liberal MP James Bryce, later Lord Bryce, President of the Alpine Club and Ambassador to the United States, and an experienced mountaineer, introduced his Access to Mountains (Scotland) Bill in 1884, it received cross-party support, prompting a thundering leader in *The Times*, and elicited supportive petitions from many Scottish cities and burghs.

But both this Bill and a successor four years later fell by the wayside, as did several other attempts at similar legislation, and today Scottish hill-goers enjoy a jealously guarded *de facto* right of access to most of the Highlands.

Ironically again, the first recorded mention of National Parks in Parliament, in 1929, also had a specifically Scottish reference. In a question to the Commissioner of Works, a Mr Macpherson called attention to the project 'of securing for the nation in perpetuity some area in the Cairngorm range or elsewhere in

Mists wreath The Three Sisters in Glen Coe, with Aonach Dubh prominent on the left

Looking across the ancient pines of Loch Maree towards the peak of Slioch, in the wilds of Wester Ross

Scotland for the free and unfettered use of the public and as a sanctuary for birds and animals'. The result was the setting up of a committee under Christopher (later Lord) Addison which, for the first time, considered the idea of National Parks in Great Britain. The Committee concluded that, while National Parks based on the American model were impossible in overcrowded Britain, there was, never the less, an 'enviable' opportunity to conserve the best of our countryside.

But when John Dower produced the blueprint for our current National Parks system in England and Wales in his 1945 Report, his terms of reference specifically excluded Scotland. He did say, however, that it was 'exceedingly desirable' that there should be National Parks in Scotland, at a rate of not less than one to three of those in England and Wales:

> The mountain masses of the Highlands, with their glens and lochs, are far larger and more continuously wild than any corresponding areas south of the Border; and (in my opinion) at least two selected Highland areas of ample size should become Scottish National Parks simultaneously with the establishment of the first six English and Welsh National Parks.

At the harbour of Kyleakin, ruined Castle Moil bares its fangs at the sky

ISLE OF SKYE

Highland

Any bonny boat speeding like a bird on the wing over to Skye is due for spectacular views of tremendous cliff scenery and the towering, ominous bulk of the Cuillin mountains. Skye's name is Norse, meaning `isle of clouds', and the south-western part of the island has some of the heaviest rainfall on the whole of the British coast. All the same, there is a powerful magic about Skye and the principal visitor attractions can become uncomfortably crowded in summer. At the moment, car ferries operate regularly to and from the mainland, but the new bridge from Kyle of Lochalsh, planned to open in 1995, has not been greeted with unmixed joy by the islanders. Skye is the largest island of the Inner Hebrides, covering some 535 square miles (1386 sq km). It is a peculiar shape, rather like a giant lobster with the claws to the north-west, and sea lochs bite deep into it, creating numerous peninsulas. The south-western one, Sleat, is known as `the garden of Skye' for the luxuriance of

Bird on the Wing
Skye cherishes the memory of the Young Pretender, Prince Charles Edward Stuart, and his escape across the Highlands after defeat at Culloden in 1746. On the tiny island of Benbecula in the Hebrides he encountered Flora Macdonald, a shapely young lady of 24, who took him `over the sea to Skye' by boat, disguised as an Irish maid named Betty Burke, and clad in a blue and white calico dress and quilted petticoat, with a cap to cover his head and face. They landed in Kilbride Bay, north of Uig, and walked to Portree, Flora amused at the immodest way in which 'Betty Burke' raised her skirts to cross streams. They said goodbye in Portree in the inn (now the Royal Hotel). The Prince spent two nights in a miserable hut on Raasay Island, then returned to Skye at a cave on the eastern shore. Now disguised as a manservant named Lewie Caw, he walked to Elgol, where the Mackenzies feasted him in another cave and sent him on by boat to Mallaig. Although there was a huge reward for his capture, the Prince was never betrayed, and eventually escaped to the Continent where he lived out his life in decaying splendour and poverty, dying in Rome in 1788.

its vegetation. At Armadale the Clan Donald Centre traces the romantic history of the Lords of the Isles, whose predatory war galleys maintained an empire in these western seas. The ruined fortress of Dunscaith crowns a headland where, according to legend, the Amazon queen Sgathach ruled long ago, and where the great Ulster hero Cuchulain came to her to be trained in warfare. To the north-west, the black, jagged and sinister peaks of the Cuillins (pronounced `Coolins'), rising to 3309 feet (1009m) in Sgurr Alasdair, are among the most dangerous mountains in Britain. Boats from Elgol penetrate to the heart of them through Loch Coruisk, possibly the most dramatic loch in all Scotland. North-west again is Dunvegan Castle, stronghold of the MacLeod chiefs in unbroken succession since the 13th century. At one time the castle could be entered only from the sea, but now a bridge lets visitors in over a ravine. Inside, besides a peculiarly horrendous dungeon, is the clan's famous fairy flag, a frail piece of tattered silk shot with gold and with crimson spots, which is unfurled in time of desperate peril. According to tradition, it was given to an early MacLeod chief by his wife, who came of the faery race. Delightful boat trips from here to Loch Dunvegan take visitors to see the seals. On the Trotternish Peninsula are the weird battlements and pinnacles of the Quiraing, one of the strangest rock formations in the country; and Flora Macdonald, heroine of the Young Pretender's escape, lies buried in the peaceful graveyard at Kilmuir. The Prince said farewell to her in Portree, on the island's eastern coast, Skye's capital and only town, which is the main touring centre today.

DUNTULM CASTLE

Isle of Skye

DUNTULM, 24 MILES (38.5 KM) NORTH OF PORTREE

This stronghold of the island clan of MacDonald stands in a commanding position overlooking a natural harbour at the extreme northern end of Skye. The rectangular tower dates from the 15th century, but a smaller tower was added in the 17th century, when the little fortress was at the height of its glory. Contemporary accounts tell of the lavish hospitality that could be enjoyed at the fine MacDonald house at Duntulm, and soil was imported from seven different countries to make the castle gardens fertile.

Several legends are attached to these atmospheric ruins. One is that the baby son of the clan chief was being dangled from a window by his nurse to see a passing ship, when she inadvertently dropped him. The chief was reported to have quit Duntulm immediately before any further misfortunes should fall on him.

A different tale involves another chief and his heir, Hugh. The story goes that Hugh was keen to inherit sooner, rather than later, and so arranged for his kinsman's murder. In an act of appalling incompetence, Hugh misaddressed his letters, sending to the chief, not the invitation to dine, but instructions to the hired killer outlining how the foul deed was to be done. Hugh was arrested and incarcerated in Duntulm's vaults with salt beef and nothing to drink. It is said that many years later a skeleton was unearthed, still clutching an empty water pitcher.

Open access at any reasonable time.

Little remains today of this former MacDonald stronghold

Dunvegan Castle has been the home of the MacLeod family for nearly 800 years

DUNVEGAN CASTLE

Isle of Skye

DUNVEGAN, 23 MILES (37 KM) WEST OF PORTREE

The story of Dunvegan Castle and its owners, the MacLeods, stretches back to the 13th century. In 1237 Leod, a son of the King of the Isle of Man and the North Isles, inherited the island of Lewis and Harris, and part of Skye. When Viking claims to the Scottish islands were finally crushed, Leod controlled a good portion of the Hebrides. He chose the rocky peninsula jutting out into the sea at Dunvegan on which to establish his fortress and headquarters. Dunvegan has remained the home of the MacLeods (meaning 'son of Leod') ever since.

Leod died in 1280, but before his death a thick wall had been built around the site, leaving only a small sea gate, through which supplies could be brought to the castle in times of siege. Between 1340 and 1360, a keep was added, which contained kitchens and a dungeon. The 'Fairy Tower' was built around 1500, while further improvements were made in the 17th century.

The entire castle was reconstructed in the 19th century, complete with noble battlements and little corner turrets, and is an impressive sight, whether approached from land or sea.

Open April to October daily. Tel: 01470 521206.

One of Dunvegan's most curious treasures is the fabled fairy flag. Modern tests have shown that this yellow silk banner dates to between AD400 and AD700, but how it came to be in the possession of the MacLeods is a mystery. There are many local legends to explain: one story tells of how it was presented to a crusader MacLeod in Palestine, while other legends insist that it was given to the family by fairies.

INDEX